D0078865

CONTINENTAL SCENE PAINTING

DESIGN BY VLADIMIR POLUNIN
FOR A DROP CURTAIN

FRONTISPIECE

THE CONTINENTAL
METHOD OF
SCENE PAINTING

By

Vladimir Polunin

Edited by
CYRIL W. BEAUMONT

Dance Books Ltd
9 Cecil Court
London WC2
1980

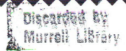
Discarded by
Murrell Library

APR 2 6 2022

Murrell Library
Missouri Valley College
Marshall, Missouri 65340

97-120

First published 1927 by C. W. Beaumont

This edition published 1980
by Dance Books Ltd
9 Cecil Court
London WC2N 4EZ

© 1980 Oleg Polunin

ISBN 0 903102 57 9

Printed and bound by
The Burlington Press (Cambridge) Ltd,
Foxton, Cambridge CB2 6SW

$29.95

91300

9-1-92 Print

To
My Wife
and Collaborator

Preface

WHEN, a few years ago, I required certain information and recipes relative to scene painting, I was considerably surprised to find that neither the library at the British Museum nor that at the Victoria and Albert Museum contained any serious works on the subject. True, there were a few volumes with promising titles, but these either completely ignored the practical side or dealt but cursorily with it. Even in the latter case they were of little practical value to me, because they concerned the painting of scenery on a frame, by the vertical method which has long ago been discontinued on the Continent, it having been supplanted by the horizontal method which offers considerable advantages both from the practical and artistic standpoints.

With the development of theatrical enterprise, the decorator ceased to be satisfied with stereotyped scenes which differed little from one another. He began to realise that each subject required its own technique, that the rendering of the individual qualities peculiar to each design, the medium in which it was painted, the *matière* and surface of the painting—in short, all the qualities that give a personal charm to an artist's work were inseparable from a correct realisation of the design to be executed. Having found this refinement impossible of attainment while working on a movable, vertical frame, Continental scene painters naturally sought new methods and so passed to painting on the floor.

At first thought, there would appear to be no difference between the two methods, for it would seem to matter little whether a scene be painted vertically on a frame, or horizontally on the floor. Practice, however, proves that the results obtained from the two methods are quite different. A certain mechanical dryness and uniformity of technique are always present in work painted by a decorator using the former method, even supposing him to be highly skilled. On the other hand, his rival is able to vary his technique at will.

Preface

Admitting the suitability of the vertical method for certain types of theatrical productions in which questions of artistic refinement do not arise, Continental decorators have become aware of the growth of the taste and artistic demands of the public which begins to prefer work which properly reproduces the ideas and peculiarities of the designer whose name figures on the programme of the performance. Executors, like easel-painters, begin to realise that the interest aroused by the work of Picasso and Bakst lies not only in their respective treatment of subjects but in their individual technical characteristics.

What, then, are the advantages of the Continental method of scene-painting ? The principal one is, that instead of a scene painted by Messrs. X. Y. & Co., the theatre direction receives one which retains the characteristics of the designer. Secondly, the horizontal method renders it possible for the decorator to employ any form of technique, from the opaque colours of tempera and gouache to the transparent washes associated with water-colour ; for, since the colours do not trickle down on a horizontal plane, the most delicate *nuances* are possible of achievement. Thirdly, the density of the priming can be varied according to the technique required. Fourthly, the decorator is able to take in at a glance the whole surface of the canvas (and not a portion only as is generally the case with work executed on a vertical frame), and work over his scene at will during the whole process of painting. This enables him to see at once the effect of the adjacent tones on each other, and facilitates the difficult task of determining the correct relation without having to hoist and lower the frame. Fifthly, cloths painted by the new method are often so thin—priming and colours included—that they can be folded like a pocket-handkerchief and dispatched all over the world in small cases. Whereas, scenes painted vertically must always be rolled on huge tumblers, for, if folded, they crack on account of their thick priming and opaque painting, drawbacks inseparable from this method. Sixthly, the resulting economy in colours, in storage and transport, is so striking that this factor alone is a strong argument in favour of the Continental method. Lastly, the decorator has no need of a special building containing huge frames and crabs, because he can paint the most complicated scenes in any large room where there is a possibility of using the floor. All these reasons prove clearly that Continental decorators did not pass from the wall to the floor for a mere whim, but on account of the manifest practical and artistic advantages to be gained.

In the last twenty years, scene painting has made enormous progress, mainly in simplifying the forms and in placing the colouring as the basis of such work. Russian decorators, working in Russia and out of it, understood the prime importance of colour-impressions for the stage. The most eminent Russian artists rushed into this captivating domain and, setting aside old traditions, achieved an artistic revolution. In this sense Diaghileff's Russian Ballet made great artistic conquests in Western Europe. To give a practical foundation to them is the purpose of this book.

Unfortunately, apprenticeship and education step by step, and day by day, in the studio of a master working in the Continental method, is practically impossible, for there are hardly any such in England. That is why a book by one who has had fifteen years' experience with the Diaghileff Company and other eminent English and Russian theatrical enterprises, may be useful, not only for workers in this branch of art in England, but for all those, too, who are interested in it on the Continent.

V. P.

LONDON, 1926.

Contents

Illustrations

Section One

TYPES OF SCENERY

HANGING scenery consists of a series of cloths hung parallel to one another and capable of being " flied " to the grid in a minimum of time. It is one of the earliest, simplest and best types of scenery and can be employed for the representation of almost any subject.

Built scenery consists of a system of flats, that is to say, canvas stretched on frames which are stood upright on the stage and set at any desired angle. This type is used generally for interiors, built architecture and sculptural masses. Such scenery well represents three dimensions, but possesses disadvantages in that it is much more expensive, difficult to set and inconvenient of transport.

In actual practice, hanging scenery is generally supplemented by a varying number of flats, while built scenery is often completed by hanging pieces.

Hanging scenery generally comprises a back-cloth and two or three cut-cloths, the number of which depends on the depth of scene required. In some cases, cut-cloths are replaced by a corresponding number of borders and pairs of separate legs or wings. Side pieces, and sometimes backing, are needed in addition for the purpose of masking in. The scene frequently includes a stage cloth and drop curtain. Certain types of scenery render it necessary for portions to be mounted on various openwork materials such as net, gauze, and so forth.

Built scenery comprises numerous flats set together, on which the relief, where required, is represented by painting. Sometimes the actual structure is built in relief, in which case the painting is reduced to a mere colouring. For example, columns built in relief will not require shading. In this type of scenery hanging pieces, such as borders, are employed chiefly to mask in the top, but very often in chamber scenes a flat will represent the ceiling for the purpose of masking in.

Stage Construction and Lighting Accommodation

The majority of stages are considerably wider than they are deep, and in height should be at least double that of their scenic cloths in order to enable them to be " flied." The proscenium opening is always smaller than the working area of the stage. If the free sides and back of the stage are too narrow it is very difficult to manipulate built scenery.

Every stage is provided with electric battens suspended from the grid and set parallel to the proscenium at a distance of from 6 to 8 feet apart, together with footlights and various other lighting contrivances.

Between these battens hang ready in position the various cloths required for the different scenes. A plan of the stage (see Plate 1) may generally be consulted in the theatre, and this will afford full details of the measurements governing the size of the scenery required and the space available for setting it.

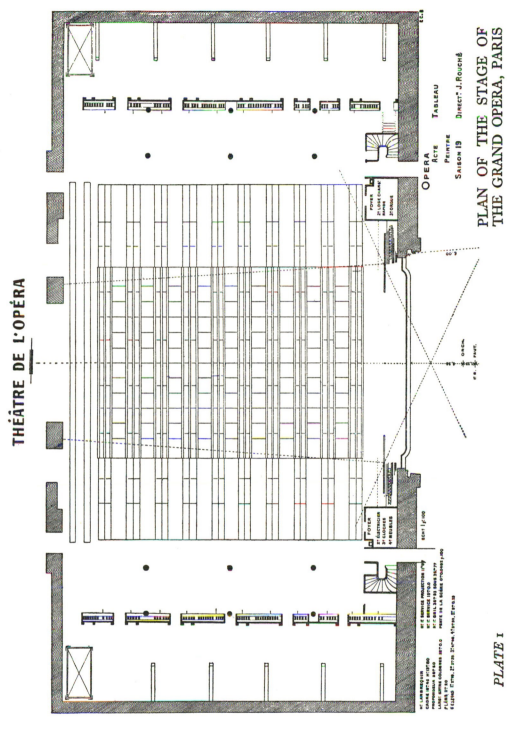

THÉÂTRE DE L'OPÉRA

OPÉRA   ACTE   TABLEAU

PEINTRE

SAISON 19   DIRECT: J. ROUCHÉ

PLAN OF THE STAGE OF
THE GRAND OPERA, PARIS

PLATE 1

If we consider the floor space in regard to the scenery required for the stages of the larger London theatres, a room 40 × 60 feet should be quite satisfactory. Again, the studio should contain a recess, lean-to, or adjoining room suitable for the storage and preparation of materials. This room must be fitted with a water supply and heating arrangements.

In short, it is inadvisable to take a studio the measurements of which both in length and breadth, are not as large as the canvas to be painted. If, however, the studio is smaller than the scenery, there are ways of meeting the consequent difficulties.[1]

Lighting

Top lighting will certainly be the best, provided that the windows extend from one wall to another, as it is essential to have an equal distribution of light on every part of the canvas. Each window should be fitted with a spring blind to screen direct sun from the floor on which the canvas is to be stretched. The disadvantage of top lighting is the intense heat that will be felt in summer time and the impossibility of preventing roof leakage during rain, one of the terrors of the scenic artist.

If top lighting is not available, side lighting is sufficient for scenic painting subject to the existence of the same facilities for equal distribution as those already mentioned. The best position for side windows is flush with the floor, in which case it is only necessary to light three sides of the studio. A combination of top and side lighting affords excellent results.

Finally, the studio must be fitted with means for artificial lighting to enable work to be continued, when necessary, at night. The best form of illuminant is ordinary electric lamps, suspended at not more than 10 feet from the floor and furnished with spreading shades, again to ensure equal distribution of the light. It will also be found advantageous to provide additional lamps capable of being moved from one part of the studio to another.

Heating and Drying Apparatus

Heating apparatus must be installed in the studio, partly for use in

---

[1] For example, if the depth of the cloth cannot be fully stretched on the floor, nail the upper portion of it and fold the lower. When the upper portion is finished and dry, roll it and then stretch and nail the lower portion.

4

the preparation of materials and partly for drying purposes. An ordinary stove or radiator, while sufficient for drying, is unsuitable for the preparation of priming, and so forth. For the latter, two or three gas rings are best, although a Primus stove can be used. Since the process of painting requires the constant preparation of priming, medium for painting, and hot water, several gas rings of different sizes are an important adjunct.

In England, drying takes generally a much longer time than on the Continent, thus causing the work to be considerably delayed. The most efficient method of drying is heat diffused by means of air currents generated by four or preferably six electric fans connected by long wires. This system of fans is particularly valuable when all are concentrated on a particular portion of the canvas which, for some inexplicable reason, has not dried with the rest. Further, colour specimens can be dried more satisfactorily by air than by heat alone.

Water Supply

A constant supply of running water, preferably both hot and cold, is imperative. The tap, whether situated in the studio or in the recess, should not be higher than 2 feet from the ground, in order to avoid splashing during the cleaning of brushes. A trough, 3×2 feet, constructed of zinc, or a large sink, approximately 6 inches deep, should be fixed on the floor underneath the tap.

Tools

The *Chalk Line* is a piece of thin, smooth cord free from knots and in length slightly exceeding that of the scenery. For use, hold it taut, rub it with charcoal, then flick the cord to make it leave a line of dust where required. Three people are best for marking, one standing in the centre to flick the cord, and one at each end to hold it taut.

A *Straight Edge* (see Plate 2, fig. 3), 6 feet in length, divided into feet and inches, and provided with a perpendicular handle, is used for speedy measuring and also for making a good edge. The bevelled edge shown in the diagram is to prevent the paint from flowing back on to the canvas.

The *Right Angle* (see Plate 2, fig. 5), which must be of exactly 45 degrees, is used for finding the central or perpendicular line and should be from 4 to 5 feet long. Some artists use the compass, which is more exact, instead of the Right Angle. This is generally 3 feet high, made of metal or wood, and fitted with a charcoal holder at one extremity and a point at the other.

The *Charcoal Holder* (see Plate 2, fig. 4), consists of a large size metal holder affixed to the end of a light bamboo cane about 3 feet 6 inches long, and is all that is necessary for drawing on the canvas. The thickness of the charcoal should correspond roughly to that of the thumb and the grain be the softest obtainable, since the harder varieties tend to mark the canvas permanently.

Sundries.

Two graduated rules, respectively of 2 and 6 feet.

A claw hammer.

Two dozen small tin pails to hold paint.

A few large pails for priming.

A quantity of gallipots or tins, also to contain paint.

A wooden paint-carrier (see Plate 10). This is easily made and indispensable.

A supply of clouts or tacks. Avoid those with sharp edges as they are apt to cut the canvas while the priming is drying. Clouts half an inch long answer all requirements.

Brushes

All brushes for painting in the Continental method must have long handles. Brushes to be held in one hand should have handles not less than 3 feet 3 inches long and be made of strong but light wood. Brushes to be held in both hands should have handles not less than 4 feet 3 inches long. The hair must be of the best quality mixed black and white bristles, soft and pliable like those of a water-colour brush.

The following is a list of the brushes of various kinds and sizes used on the Continent :—

One-hand Brushes.

(1) Size $2\frac{1}{2} \times 1\frac{1}{2}$ inches, with bristles $4\frac{1}{2}$ inches long set in four rows of five bunches (see Plate 2, fig. 1).

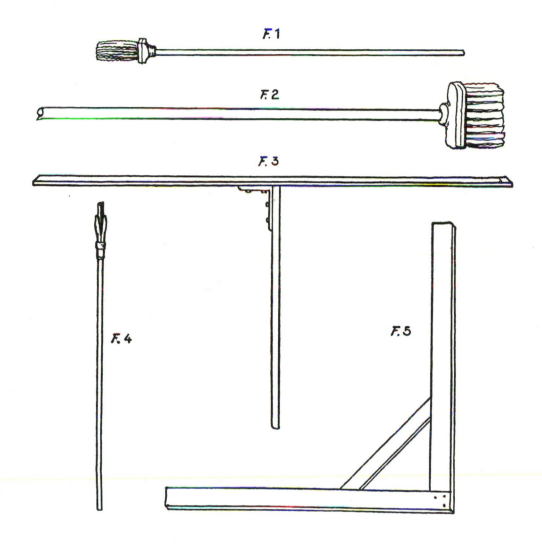

F. 1

F. 2

F. 3

F. 4

F. 5

Fig. 1. One Hand Brush.   Fig. 2. Two Hand
Brush.   Fig. 3. Straight Edge.   Fig. 4. Charcoal Holder.   Fig. 5. Right Angle.

PLATE 2

(2) Round brush, about $2\frac{1}{2}$ inches in diameter and with bristles $4\frac{1}{2}$ inches long.

(3) Outline brush, size $1 \times \frac{1}{2}$ inch, with bristles $4\frac{1}{2}$ inches long, bound together.

Two-hand Brushes.

(1) Priming Brush. The best size is 8×4 inches, with bristles 5 inches long. The quantity of bristles should be approximately eight rows of sixteen bunches, but a priming brush measuring $5\frac{1}{2} \times 2\frac{1}{2}$ inches, with six rows of ten bunches of bristles is quite service-able. A brush of this size can also be used for the painting of large flat tones (see Plate 2, fig. 2).

(2) Size $4\frac{1}{2} \times 2$ inches, with bristles $4\frac{1}{2}$ inches long, arranged in bunches.

(3) Flat brushes, size $4\frac{1}{2}$ inches $\times$ 1 inch, with bristles $3\frac{1}{2}$ inches long bound together.

All the above-mentioned are obtainable at the best Paris scenic brush makers. Some short-handled English brushes of various shapes and sizes are excellent, and can easily be screwed on to long handles. With the addition of a few artist's brushes which can be fixed in the charcoal holder, the articles necessary for the painting of scenery will be complete.

The Care of Brushes

At the end of the day's work the brushes must be washed thoroughly in warm water, and either hung upside down or placed flat on the ground to prevent damage to the bristles. It is a mistake to leave the brushes in water, since this tends to make the bristles hard and brittle. Some Russian artists leave their brushes in priming paste. This is a good practice for it keeps the bristles very soft. When travelling, or during periods of inactivity, it is best to keep the brushes in a long, specially made box, but they must be perfectly dry before being put away.

Canvas

The choice of canvas is influenced to some extent by the technique required by the design in question. If the designer requires a water-colour effect it will be best to choose the ordinary white scenic canvas manufactured in England. If, however, the sketch is in *gouache* or body colour, a coarse canvas is preferable, in which case French makes are the most economical and suitable.

Great care should be exercised in the selection of canvas. The threads should be inspected in both directions to ascertain whether they are of equal strength, of the same material and closely woven. The latter quality of canvas is best because, owing to the texture being finer, the priming holds better and the light on the stage does not show through from the back, an important factor when thin priming is used. To test the strength of the material, endeavour to tear a small piece of the edge of the canvas ; if this cannot be achieved in either direction, it may be regarded as strong enough. It is astonishing how easy it is to tear with the fingers the apparently stout canvases of French manufacture. Prior to the war the best canvas was that manufactured in Russia. The width of the canvas is important, the wider it is the better since it lessens the number of seams and saves the expense of sewing. Canvas heavily dressed should be avoided, for, when it is used, a white powder appears on the surface.

Fireproof and Fireproofing

The necessity for treating materials used on the stage to ensure precaution against fire is obvious, but the fact remains that fireproofed canvas is a nightmare to scenic artists of all methods. First, it changes and sometimes quite destroys the colours (particularly gold, blue and certain reds), especially when the painting has been carried out in the Continental method, which requires delicate priming and medium. Secondly, many unpleasant surprises distress both the inexperienced and even the experienced. These surprises vary according to the particular fireproof solution with which the canvas has been treated, and since these recipes are trade secrets it is very difficult to guard against injury. The least dangerous are the solutions prepared by the P.P. Fireproofing Company, and Lomax. One pound of solution diluted with a gallon of water is a suitable mixture for applying with a spraying machine or brush. When selecting fireproofed canvas beware of that which is damp to the touch, very salt to the taste, and patchy in appearance.

If it is desired to fireproof scenery already painted, the solution must be applied to the back of the canvas, whether it is sprayed or brushed. If sprayed on, the solution dries in patches, while if brushed on canvas laid face downwards on the floor the result is even worse, for pressure on the wet canvas causes the paint to come off in patches on to the floor. There are many controversies on the subject of fire-proofing, but everyone agrees that both methods are unsatisfactory. But for scenery to be used in England it is on the whole better to paint on canvas which has been already fire-proofed some time before it is to be used.

Sewing of Canvas

The first point to remember is that the cut strips of canvas must hang horizontally. They may be sewn together either by hand or by machine, the former method being best, but slow and costly. If, however, this is possible, the seams must be oversewn on the back with strong thread, first pinning carefully to avoid one part stretching further than antici-pated. This must be done by experienced workers, as uneven sewing will cause puckers in the material. The advantages of machine sewing are economy of time and expense and the fact that the work can be executed by any careful sempstress, but it should be remembered that thread again must be used and every seam finished by hand, otherwise if one stitch parts the whole seam will split.[1] When the sewing is completed, each seam must be stretched by pulling and the cloth folded inwards. Sometimes pockets are required both at the top and bottom of the cloths. Such a pocket is made by turning over 6 inches of the cloth and stitching it down, this provides a bag for the batten to pass through.

Sweeping and Cleaning the Floor

It is imperative to sweep the floor thoroughly and remove all clouts, dust, etc., before laying the canvas, as it is impossible to remove any

---

[1] On one occasion the Swan Princess Scene in *Contes Russes* caught at one end and split in two, fortunately just at the fall of the drop curtain.

harmful object afterwards. Do not forget that you will walk many miles over the canvas before your work is completed and, if clouts are left and trodden on, holes will result, while the dust carried by your shoes from the corners of the studio will be transferred to the painted surface.

Stretching the Canvas

Place the cloth on the floor with the sewing face downwards and smooth it out as well as you can. Mark a distinct line with your chalk line on the boards at the top of the canvas and carefully adjust the selvedge or pocket edge so that it coincides with this line. Next, commencing from the middle, smooth, but do not stretch, the canvas each way, nailing as you go. The clouts should be set 4 to 6 inches apart in a horizontal line and at a distance of nearly 1 inch from the edge, and be neither driven home nor loose. Now arrange the cloth by pulling it gently and mark a perpendicular chalk line on the boards (near the shorter sides of the cloth) with the help of the right angle at each end of the horizontal line already marked, placing nails temporarily at the extremity of each seam. Mark off on these perpendicular lines the length of the canvas when stretched. Join these two points by a chalk line, to which gently pull and nail the canvas starting from the centre. Complete the nailing on one side, removing the temporary nails at the seam if necessary. Now pass to the opposite side, stretch the canvas strongly and nail firmly. Look up each seam and if they are straight the canvas will have been stretched correctly. If this has not been done properly, correct from the sides only, as the top and bottom edges must remain fixed. The operation of stretching (*see* Plate 3) requires two men at least and demands great care.

Priming

Each country and each individual artist makes use of different priming. That in general use by English scene painters consists of size and whiting, which dries very quickly, but deadens the colour and is inclined to crack when folded. Scenery painted on canvas primed in this way must be rolled on tumblers which are very inconvenient for transport.

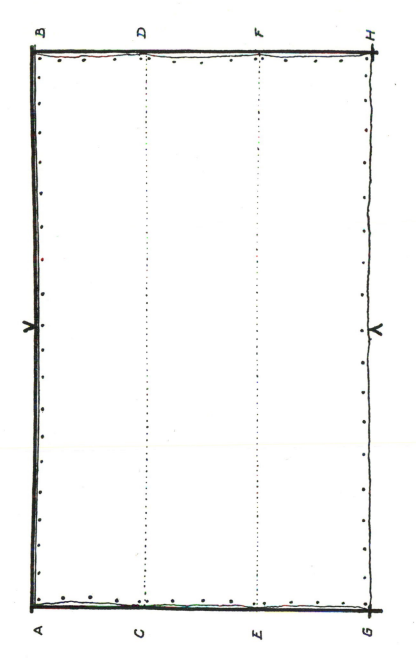

METHOD OF STRETCHING
THE CANVAS

A B. Horizontal Chalk Line.
A G. & B H. Perpendicular Chalk Lines.
G H. Base of Canvas.   C D & E F. Seams.

PLATE 3

The Process of Scene Painting in the Continental Method

Continental artists, French for example, employ a priming made of *Colle de Peau* mixed with *Blanc de Meudon*. This is not so thick as the English priming, is a little more pliable, but also inclined to dull the colour. Russian primings are various, but alike in their thinness and flexibility and do not affect the colour. Scenery so primed can be folded like a handkerchief and packed into wooden cases for transit. All the scenes used by the Diaghileff Company are packed in cases about 3 × 5 × 3 feet, one being sufficient to contain several scenes. The enormous practical advantage of this priming is obvious.

For Russian priming prepare a paste made from good plain flour and water. Add dissolved French glue [1] in proportion to suit your work. This priming is excellent for bright or very delicate painting, and will afford a silky surface on which to paint, but has the disadvantage of being very sensitive to fireproof. Here is another recipe, less affected by fireproofing. Take your paste and add a sufficient quantity of size ($\frac{3}{4}$ lb. concentrated powdered size to 2 gallons of water), mix well together and the priming is ready.

Process of Continental Priming

Prepare a quantity of priming sufficient for the whole cloth since, should a further supply become necessary, difficulty will be found in making it up to the same consistency and the cloth will be unevenly primed, a defect which will not only cause the cloth to hang badly in the theatre, but make the painting more difficult.

For a cloth 50 × 30 feet, of smooth English canvas prepare two large pails of lukewarm priming. A coarse canvas requires almost double this amount.

Sweep the canvas to remove all dust and fluff.

Take the largest priming brush, and, starting from the top left-hand corner, work in narrow strips towards the top right-hand corner. Take care that the brush is not overcharged with priming, for this tends to unevenness. Work the priming well into the grain of the canvas as

---

[1] Take care that this is made from transparent cakes of French glue and not carpenter's Scotch glue.

evenly as possible, finishing with a horizontal sweep of the brush. This affords a pleasant, uniform surface.

As the process of priming takes a considerable time, instruct your apprentice to follow behind you, as shown in Plate 4, and see that he works the priming particularly well into the seams. Two experienced men can complete a large cloth in an hour.

Drying

Priming should be carried out at the end of the day's work, so that the cloth may be dry by the following morning.

In England drying takes much longer than on the Continent owing to the moisture in the air and the fireproofing in the canvas. In Paris a primed cloth will dry thoroughly in half a day in summer ; in Monte Carlo in even less time. In England, during the winter period of fogs, a primed cloth may not dry for several days, hence heating and drying arrangements are necessary.

Supposing the priming to have been done at night, examine the cloth on your return to the studio next morning. If it is still damp and lies in creases there is no need to be discouraged, the cloth will stretch taut when thoroughly dry. If the cloth is quite dry and still shows creases, it is proof that the priming was too weak or that the canvas was insufficiently stretched. Should the canvas be nearly dry and the creases very bad, remove a few nails at a time from the sides of the cloth and carefully stretch it, but this cannot be done once the canvas is quite dry. If the cloth is stretched like a drum-head, of an even colour, does not peel when lightly scratched and is soft to the touch, you may conclude that your priming is ideal.

Pay great attention to priming or its deficiencies will be made apparent to you during every hour of your painting. Insufficient or poor priming also prevents the cloth from hanging well in the theatre.

Design

Practically any design can be used for the purpose of scenery, but not every design can be translated into terms of good scenery. Certain

THE PROCESS OF PRIMING

PLATE 4

rudiments of stage requirements must be understood by the designer to ensure good results. The sketch must give a clear idea of the construction and colour scheme of the scenery desired. When the designer and executor are one and the same person—this is ideal—he will plan his design always bearing in mind his stage requirements. If the executor is another person, he may have great difficulty in realising the designer's intentions unless he can see at once from the design of how many planes the scene will consist, and how the stage lighting will affect the general colour scheme. The difficulty consists in that the designer, not being experienced in stage limitations, although he may be a great artist as regards the painting of easel pictures, will require from the executor many impossible or ineffective qualities. In such cases, it is far better for the designer to consult the executor in regard to his plans, so that he can produce a practical design. For example, a sketch designed without knowledge of the proportions of the stage in question, cannot result in scenery which will afford complete satisfaction. Similar misunderstandings can arise in regard to the general tone and stage lighting, the dissimilarity between the designer's medium and the colours used by the scenic artist, and the frequent over-elaboration of the sketch.

The *Maquette* or Model

In the majority of cases, a suitable sketch is all that is required, but some artists prefer to work from a built model or a flat *maquette*. It is true that a model affords a clear idea of the construction and of the masking in of the scenery on the stage, but, if such a model is coloured and considered sufficient without the need of a sketch in addition, the executor may find difficulty in realising the colour scheme.

A *maquette*, or flat model, is a booklet of which each page represents a plane of the scene. This also explains the manner of construction, but does not deal with the masking in. It is convenient to work from such a booklet which is simply a coloured version of the working sketches which must be prepared for each plane of a scene before the canvas can be painted.

13

The Preparation of Working Drawings

Before planning your working drawings consider how best to divide your sketch according to the planes of the scenery. For example, should the design represent a garden (see Plate 8) and be drawn to scale, and the producer not require much space, it is sufficient to have three planes, a back-cloth and two cut-cloths, or, in place of the latter, two pairs of wings and two borders.

Place over the sketch a piece of fine tracing paper of similar size, and trace only those parts which you are to paint on the back-cloth. Observe that the two sides and a narrow strip at top and bottom of your tracing paper are blank. Consider carefully what imaginary line on the tracing will correspond to the bottom of the back-cloth. Mark this line, bearing in mind that the horizon line of the scene should not be more than 4 feet from the bottom of the cloth. When this base line is distinctly drawn, fill in the sides and top of the tracing paper with a drawing in the character of the design. You now have the complete tracing for your back-cloth (*see* Plate 7).

Take a new piece of tracing paper of the same size for your *second* cut-cloth (that is the one nearest the back-cloth), and trace what you can of this second plane, filling in the sides and top in the same character as before (*see* Plate 6). Then take a third piece of tracing paper for the first cut-cloth and trace what you can see for this. This brings you to the extreme limits of the sketch, but this again may need to be continued outwards in the character of the design, according to the size of the theatre (*see* Plate 5). The tracings are now complete.

Should you decide on wings and borders in preference to cut-cloths, the procedure will be the same except that it will be necessary to continue the tops of the wings and the sides of the borders in the general character of the design. If you are inexperienced or in doubt as to the suitability of your drawings, trace the three planes on to card-board, cut out the inner outlines of the cut-cloths, and fix them in the relative position they would occupy on the stage. This will afford a complete idea in miniature of the whole. You can now lower or raise the horizon line by cutting away or adding to the bottom of the back-cloth and make any other corrections necessary. This

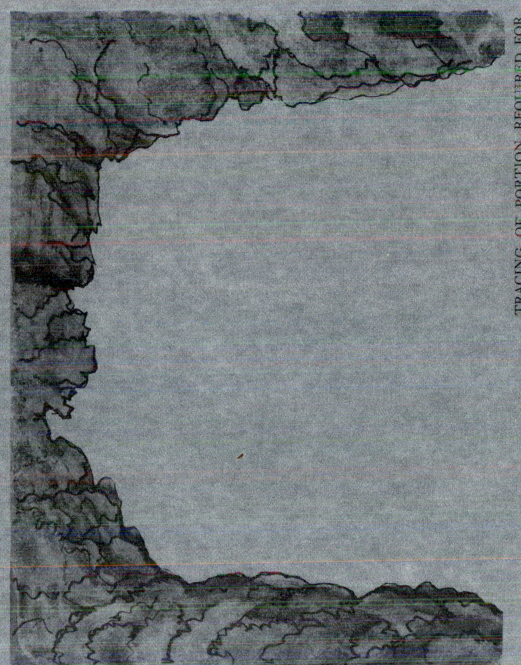

TRACING OF PORTION REQUIRED FOR
FIRST CUT-CLOTH OF *LES SYLPHIDES*

PLATE 5

PLATE 2

TRACING OF PORTION REQUIRED FOR
FIRST CUT-CLOTH OF THE SYLLABLES

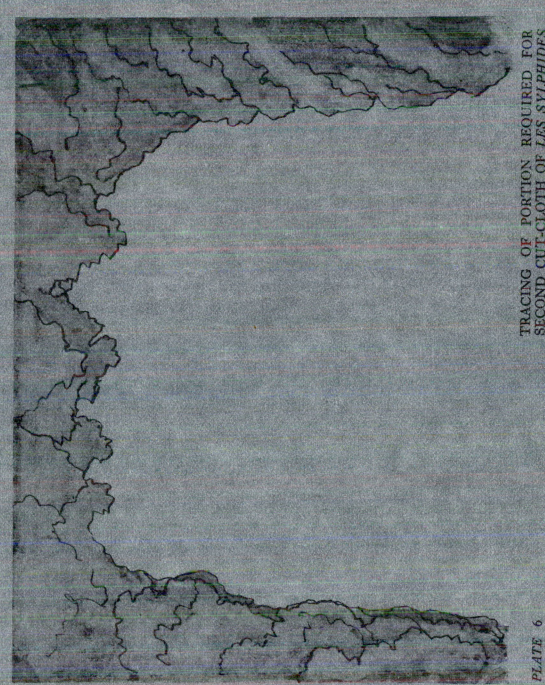

TRACING OF PORTION REQUIRED FOR
SECOND CUT-CLOTH OF *LES SYLPHIDES*

PLATE 6

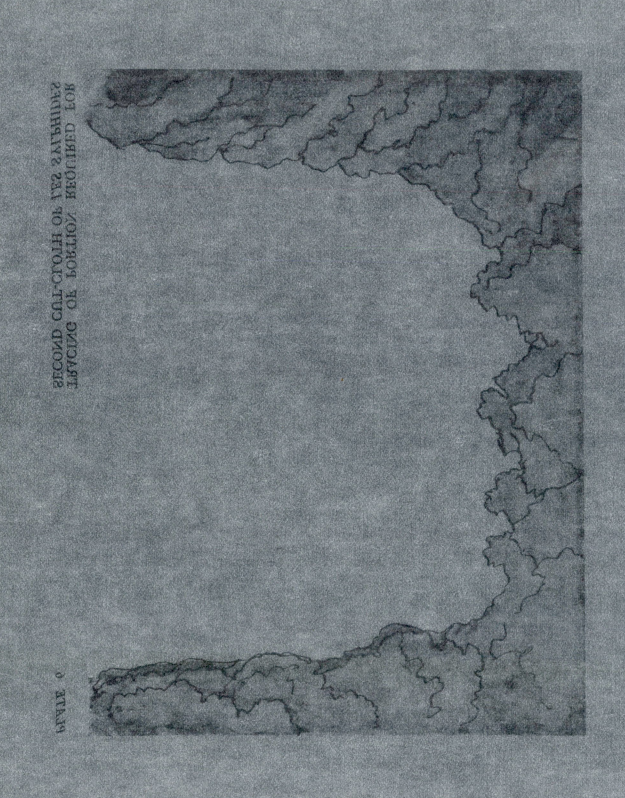

TRACING OF PORTION REQUIRED
SECOND CUT-GROIN OF LES SAUVAGES

PLATE 6

METHOD OF LINING PORTION OF
DESIGN REQUIRED FOR BACK-CLOTH

PLATE 7

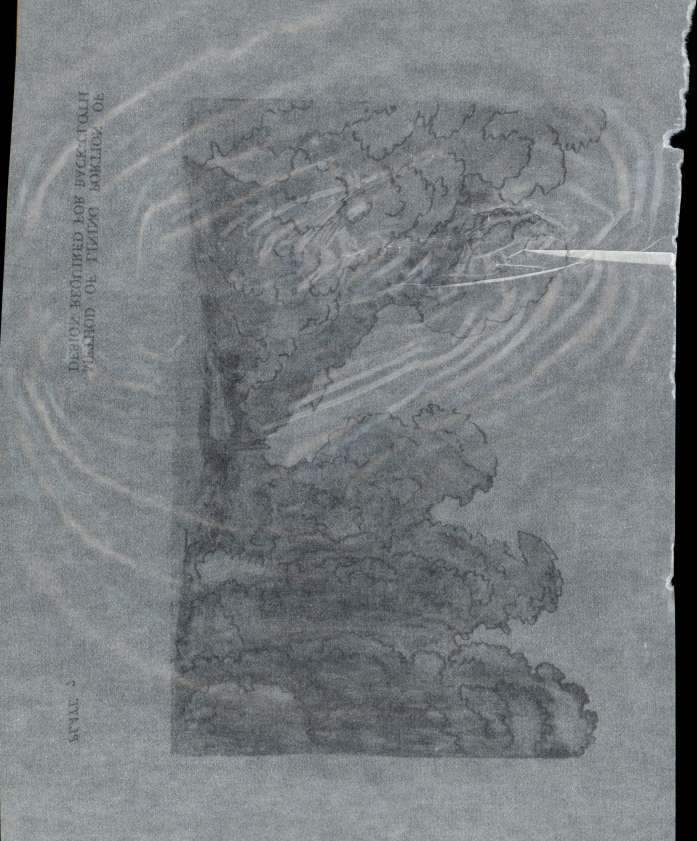

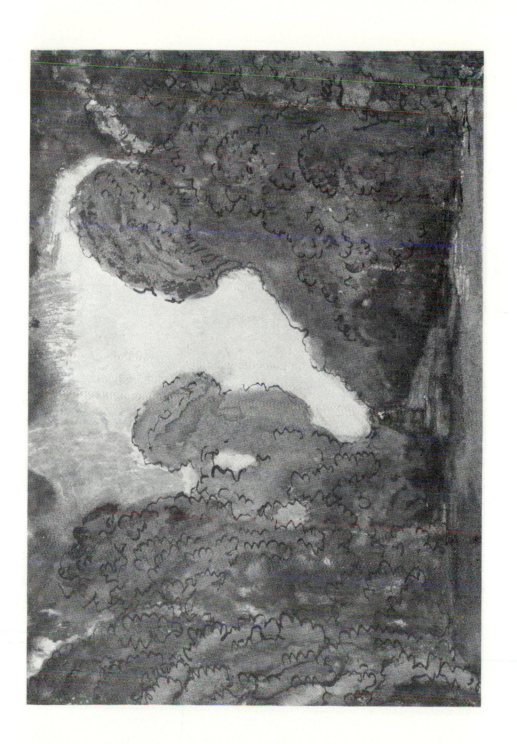

DESIGN BY VLADIMIR POLUNIN
FOR *LES SYLPHIDES*

PLATE 8

should be done by instinct rather than by rule of thumb. It will also be possible to note whether your scenery masks in at the sides and top. For example, if the top edge of the back-cloth is visible through the second cut-cloth, it is proof that you have cut away too much at the top of the latter. Add a piece as required, or, if the second cut-cloth obscures too much of the back-cloth, cut it away where necessary.

Similarly correct your first cut-cloth in regard to the second.

With regard to the side edges of your cloth, it will be found that usually side wings are required. The drawings for these should be roughly a repetition of the sides of the cloth for which they are intended.

Do not omit to correct your tracings from your cardboard planes.

If your design represents a complicated architectural scene the principles of tracing are the same as described already, but you will require some knowledge of general and stage perspective which you will find treated briefly in the following works : Lloyd (F.), *Practical Guide to Scene Painting*, 1875 ; and Atkinson (F.), *Scene Painting*, 1923.

Preparation of Working Drawing

Take the tracing of the back-cloth, note the line which is to represent the bottom of the back-cloth, and find the exact centre of it. Now erect a perpendicular from that point to the top of the drawing which gives the important central line from which all the squaring measurements will be taken.

Suppose the measurements of the back-cloth are to be 48 feet long by 30 feet high. Divide the area representing the back-cloth into yard squares in the following manner. Start, using a scale suitable to the size of the tracing paper, from the central line, and mark off 8 equal divisions on the left half of the base line and the same number on the right half. Now erect a perpendicular from the last point on each side, the height corresponding with that of the central line. Mark off 10 divisions, equal in size to those on the base line, on each of these side perpendiculars. Join these points. Now mark off 8 equal divisions on the left half of the top line and the same number on the right half. Join these points to those immediately opposite in the base line. The number of squares on the sketch will correspond to the number of yard squares required on the cloth. Mark the central perpendicular line at its top and base with 0 and 0, and number the squares to right and left of the central line and also up the sides, as shown in Plate 9. Repeat this procedure on each tracing.

The working drawings are now ready for transference to the canvas. All this is simple, provided the height and width of the sketch are in proportion to those of the stage for which the scenery is intended.

Squaring up Canvas

Return to the canvas which is dry and tempting. Take the chalk line and make a distinct line just above the bottom of the canvas, parallel and close to its edge. Find the exact centre of this line with the rule or straight-edge, place the right angle on this point, and erect a perpendicular by means of the chalk line. Take great care that this central line is placed correctly, otherwise the drawing of the whole cloth will be crooked.

Now proceed on the canvas as in the tracing, that is, starting from the central line, mark off 8 equal divisions, each of 1 yard, on the left half of the base line and the same number on the right half. Now erect a perpendicular from the last point on each side, and mark off on each 10 divisions equal in size to those on the base line. Join these points. Now mark off 8 divisions, each of 1 yard, on the left half of the top line and an equal number on the right half. Join these points to those immediately opposite in the base line. If the last division falls exactly on the side line the cloth is correctly squared, failing which, either the central line is not placed correctly, or the divisions are inexact. Find out the reason for the error and correct immediately. Number the squares to correspond with those in the drawing. The squared canvas is now a large scale copy of the squared tracing.

Drawing on the Canvas

Now, with your tracing in one hand and charcoal holder in the other, begin drawing in one of the top squares exactly what is contained in the corresponding square of the tracing. Fill in the square adjoining, and continue until all the squares are completed. Now mount the

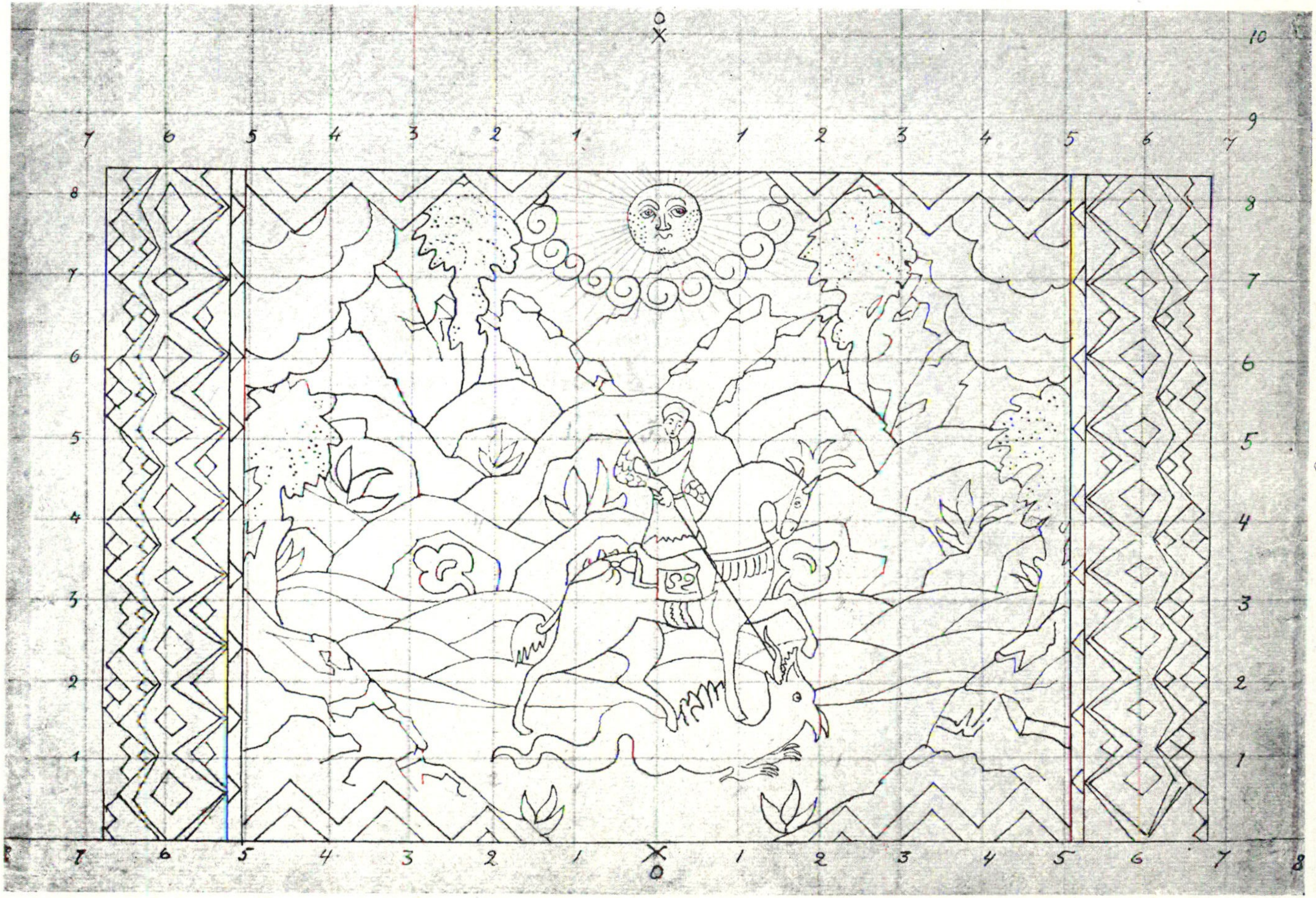

METHOD OF SQUARING TRACING
OF DESIGN FOR TRANS-
FERENCE TO THE CANVAS

PLATE 9

ladder, and you will obtain a bird's-eye view of your drawing. Carefully examine it from several points of view to ascertain if the drawing on the canvas represents the same characteristic lines contained in the tracing. If it fails to do so, it is proof that you have allowed the detail to break up the important lines of the design. Correct, always bearing in mind that in scenery it is the general effect that is essential. If you are pressed for time, and this is frequently the case in scene painting, cut the tracing in two and give half to your apprentice who can execute his share sufficiently well provided you do not omit to overlook it when finished and bring the chief lines into character with your own.

If your apprentice has difficulty in placing the lines in his squares, furnish him with a scale measure and foot rule ; he will soon discover how to avoid mistakes in measurement. A capable apprentice is quite competent to undertake the whole of the drawing himself while you prepare the colours, but do not forget to examine his work.

Simplification of Drawing

If the designer's sketch is very complicated, it is advisable to simplify the tracing, choosing the most characteristic lines and masses, for it is easy to lose oneself in a maze of lines on the canvas. It is a distinct aid to indicate the shadows very lightly and then leave the drawing in order to concentrate on the colour scheme.

Colours Used in Scene Painting

Pigments.—These are the same for water colour, oil colour, distemper, and so on, the name varying according to the medium or vehicle used. If pigment powder is ground and mixed with oil, it is known as oil colour. The same powder mixed with glue or size is termed distemper, which is used for scene painting. The dry colouring matter is of the same origin as that used for the painting of easel pictures, but it is less finely ground, of an inferior quality, and generally adulterated with other substances to enable it to be sold at a low price—an important factor on account of the large quantity required for the painting of a single scene. It is well, however, to beware of exceptionally cheap colours, for they often fade with astonishing rapidity, particularly those of an attractively brilliant hue.

French colours, which are remarkable for their brilliancy, fade quickly and unevenly. English colours, though duller in appearance, are more permanent and fade uniformly, a matter of importance, since the general effect of the scene will be retained.

A List of Useful Colours

White.—Zinc white is preferable, since it combines well with other colours, does not present the chalky effect of other whites, is comparatively transparent, and adheres closely to the canvas. Flake white has much more body, and so can be employed in those parts which require a high light.

Earth colours are preferable to all others on account of their permanence of tone, purity and adhesive qualities. The following are the most useful :—

Yellow Ochre, a good even colour, but which dries lighter, and is somewhat chalky.

Raw Sienna.—An excellent colour, which in many cases can be used to advantage in place of Yellow Ochre.

Burnt Sienna.—A good concentrated colour which affords delicate shades when combined with Zinc White.

Raw Umber.—A beautiful colour which dries lighter, but is not chalky.

Burnt Umber.—A good deep colour, useful for contrasts.

Vandyke Brown.—A fine colour when used thinly, and transparent.

Terre Verte.—A beautiful, delicate colour, but rarely used by scene painters, and, therefore, difficult to obtain.

English Red.—A fine colour, but difficult to procure for scene painting in particularly good quality.

Mineral and Other Colours

Chromes (Light, Medium and Deep).—These are brilliant colours which, however, must be used rather thickly, and have a tendency to become dull and dirty in course of time. They should not be combined with other colours.

Red Lead.—A fine orange colour, but very heavy.

Vermillion.—An expensive but concentrated colour, which is equally good whether applied thinly or thickly, and covers evenly.

Vermillionette (Pale and Deep).—These colours are rather unsatisfactory especially when used thinly. They are frequently employed, however, on account of their low price.

Carnation Paste.—A fine concentrated colour which adheres firmly to the canvas. It can be used either thickly or thinly.

Damp Lake.—A colour which is dull, weak, and dries patchily. It is often used in place of the above on account of its low price.

Leather Lake.—A beautiful shade, especially when used thinly.

Mauve Lake.—A very concentrated colour which adheres well.

Blues

Ultramarine (French).—A very important and largely used colour. It is brilliant, but possesses a tendency to fade to grey, particularly when combined with impure pigment. It has the worst adhesive quality of any pigment, and consequently requires a strong medium.

Azure Blue.—A good colour which can be used to replace cobalt.

Indigo.—A wonderful colour used thinly or thickly, but difficult to procure.

Prussian Blue.—A delightful colour when used thinly, but dries patchily when thick.

Daylight Blue, *Night Blue*, *Damp Blue.*—These colours are for use in special cases only.

Greens

Viridian.—A beautiful, pure and concentrated colour, but expensive.

Emerald Green.—A most brilliant colour, but possessing many disadvantages ; it does not combine well with its medium, adheres badly, covers unevenly, and dries patchily and lighter.

Brunswick Greens (Middle, Deep and Blue).—These colours are dull and weak, adhere badly, but brush evenly, and are low-priced.

Bronze Greens (Pale, Middle, and Deep).—These colours have a tendency to become muddy.

Blacks

Ivory Black.—An excellent colour whether used thinly or thickly, which affords beautiful shades with Zinc White, Terre Verte and other pigments. If used thickly, it must be combined with extra strong medium to prevent its falling off.

Gold and Silver Powders

These powders are obtainable in varying shades, but must generally be used sparingly. They can be mixed with each other, and even, if desired, with pigments. They require special mediums.

Mediums for Scenic Painting

If you have prepared your priming from paste and glue in the manner already described, take glue for your medium. Break up with a hammer a few cakes of transparent French glue and soak them in a small quantity of water for about twenty-four hours. When the glue is softened, add water to bring it to the strength you require for painting and pour it into a double saucepan over a low heat. Stir the solution from time to time taking care not to allow it to boil. This should result in an excellent transparent and flexible medium capable of affording a water-colour effect where necessary, and of giving a silky surface to the canvas.

Very often fireproof does not agree with glue, so that the great advantages of this medium become a source of trouble. Again, it is difficult to maintain the solution in the same consistency for, as it is kept on the stove for many hours, it becomes more concentrated, so that it is difficult to judge when there is sufficient and not an excess of glue to hold the pigments ; also, it soon decomposes when combined with them. Extensive practice alone can inform you which colours need concentrated or weak medium.

Remember that Ultramarine, Ivory Black, Emerald Green, Sienna and a few other colours require nearly double strength medium, and if this is over concentrated, there is a danger of your having a muddy dark colour with a tendency to shine, crack and peel. But despite all these drawbacks, French glue is one of the best of mediums, and scenery painted with it will look fresh and bright ten and even fifteen years later.

If you have selected *Colle de Peau* combined with *Blanc de Meudon* for the priming, use *Colle de Peau* as your medium, warming it without the addition of water. This results in *Colle entière*.

Take a large vessel, add hot water to the *Colle entière* in the proportion of three to six parts of the former to one of the latter, according to your requirements. Keep this medium always warm and ready for use. This is a good and convenient medium which can easily be reheated both by itself and when mixed with pigment, without affecting the strength of the *Colle de Peau*.

For those colours which require a stronger medium add a little *Colle entière* to the paint. *Colle de Peau* is a convenient medium with which to work, and is less affected by fireproofed canvas than the one described previously, but is not without disadvantages; for example, the painted surface becomes duller than when executed with glue medium, and is less flexible.

If the priming consists of size and paste, size will be the medium for painting. Take two-thirds of a pound of concentrated powdered size and completely dissolve it in a little cold water, stirring it carefully. When dissolved add boiling water to make 2 gallons of the mixture. Bring it again to the boil and allow to cool when it is ready for use.

Size medium is convenient in use, retains a uniform strength, combines readily with the pigment, is no trouble to reheat, keeps the colour bright and agrees more or less well with fireproof, but is rougher and not so pliable as glue medium.

Aniline Dyes and Painting with Aniline Colour

If the scenery requires plain surfaces of thin colour, or if it is desired to afford a silky surface to the canvas (for example, in the case of the representation of curtains and other hangings) use aniline dye. The process of dyeing for stage purposes is quite straightforward.

Dissolve the grains of aniline in warm water to the strength desired, add a little Glauber's salt to the solution as a mordant, and dip the canvas in the solution, moving it about continually. As soon as it is the required colour, take the material out with the help of your apprentice and hang it up to dry, avoiding creases. When dry, it will be as soft as a handkerchief, for remember that canvas to be dyed with aniline must not be primed.

Should a transparent effect be required in the scenery when a light is placed behind some part of it, dye or paint in aniline on fine special linen.

Instead of dipping the material in aniline, the dye may be applied with a large soft brush, the canvas being previously nailed to the floor. The slight natural unevenness of surface resulting from the use of the brush affords a pleasant silky effect, particularly beautiful in folds.

If it is required to paint a pattern in aniline, it is necessary to add to the solution a special medium for fixing the aniline and to prevent the excessive running of the colours. This medium is expensive, as its chemical composition is a trade secret. Aniline is particularly useful for the colouring of materials for costumes and properties. It is valuable on account of its brilliancy, strength of colour, flexibility, transparency and adhesiveness, but, on the other hand, it fades rapidly and unevenly, and is difficult to retouch.[1] Again, it is brilliant only when used pure, a mixture of two or more colours losing in brilliancy and sometimes even becoming dirty in tone.

Actual Painting

Colour Test.—Before preparing the necessary pigments, consider carefully the colour scheme of the design. If it is a landscape in water-colour, and it is desired to reproduce this effect, prepare the general tones and mix them with sufficient medium. Try them one after another on a strip of canvas primed in the same manner as the cloth to

---

[1] *Cléopâtre*, designed by Delaunay, and the Bedchamber Scene in Verdi's *Otello*, designed by V. Polunin, are examples of scenery painted completely in aniline.

be painted and ascertain whether the colours both separately and together correspond to those in the design. Notice, also, whether the paints adhere firmly to the canvas. It will often be found that while the tones appear true when examined separately, they appear lacking when regarded in relation to one another or as a whole. This is caused by the deflection of light produced by the grain in the canvas, the coarser quality of scenic pigments, and the medium with which they are mixed. Slightly vary some of the individual colours until you are assured that the general harmony of the colour tests is the same as that of the design.[1] These comparisons and tests should be carried out with the greatest care and deliberation. Put all your knowledge and experience into the preparation of the colours, or later there will be many corrections to make on the cloth under much more difficult conditions and with the certain loss of freshness in the painting. Freshness of colour and lightness of touch are all important in the painting of scenery.

Now prepare sufficient colour for the painting of the cloth, and more than sufficient of the colours which are to be repeated on the cutcloths. Number your pails according to the gradation of the colours they contain in order to avoid the possibility of mistakes due to working in artificial light. Mark distinctly the top centre of the cloth with paint and sweep the canvas carefully. Place your sketch so that you can consult it from a distance while at work, and begin painting from the top of the canvas, making sure that the brushes have previously been thoroughly washed. Begin to paint as though you were making an enormous sketch in water-colour, applying the colours very wet, and allowing them to run freely into one another where desirable. The lines already made on the canvas will mark the boundaries of the colours, but if the brush carries the colour beyond it by an inch or two, it will not be noticeable. At this point the whole attention must be concentrated on attaining the general colour effect and character of the sketch, and not on the accuracy of the drawing.

It will often be found during painting that further gradations of

---

[1] There is no harm in slightly intensifying the tints of the tests, since the same tones used in large quantities on the canvas usually dry lighter than in the trials.

colour are needed, hence there must be kept ready to hand a pail of clean water in which the brush can be dipped in order to weaken the tone. Try to cover the whole of the canvas during the day so that on resuming operations next morning the detail can be painted in and a second coat applied on to a dry surface. Take the sketch in hand, and endeavour to obtain a bird's-eye view of your work to ascertain whether the general effect corresponds to that of the sketch. If it does not do so, repaint any false tones, always remembering that when the same colour is applied as a second coat it will be much more intense than the first. Once the general effect is achieved there will be no risk of its being destroyed when you proceed to add any necessary details and delicacies of tone. Even inaccurate detail will pass unnoticed among its immense surroundings of harmonious tone.

Since the charm of water-colour consists in its delicate technique and peculiar surface, do not ignore its characteristics. For example, should some of the dark tones be too heavy, never try to lighten them with the aid of white. Take a soft sponge previously rinsed out in clean water and wipe off what is not required.[1] With practice, beautiful water-colour effects can be obtained in this manner.[2]

Whenever possible, examine your work by artificial light. In general, the effect will be more harmonious, and the colours found to be little changed with the exception of mauves which appear duller and certain yellows which look lighter than required. Correct the colour by artificial light.

Subject every part of the cloth to severe criticism, but train yourself to know when to leave off, since each further correction lessens the freshness of the final effect.

The most important part of the scenery, the back-cloth, is finished.

Take number 2 cut-cloth (*i.e.*, the one nearest the back-cloth), and proceed in the same manner as before, that is, stretch a full-sized cloth, prime, square, draw, paint and correct it. When it is finished and thoroughly dry, cut away the unpainted surface; the central piece of

---

[1] As in the central hills in Derain's drop curtain for *La Boutique Fantasque ;* also the waves and hills in the *Russian Ballet* drop curtain designed by V. Polunin.

[2] *Les Femmes de Bonne Humeur*, designed by Bakst, and *Le Beau Danube*, designed by V. Polunin, are examples of scenery painted from sketches in water-colour.

Photo : Graphic]

PLATE 10

CONTINENTAL METHOD OF
PAINTING THE CLOTH
STRETCHED ON THE FLOOR

unused canvas will be found useful later on for side pieces, flats, and so on.

Now stretch number 1 cut-cloth and proceed similarly, but bear in mind that since this is nearest the audience, it must receive particular attention. With the painting of the flats and side pieces, which are merely used for the purpose of masking in, the scenery will be complete.

Now let us suppose that the original design is executed in *gouache*, tempera or other body colour. Here, contrary to water-colour, the lighter tones may be painted on the top of the darker. Since this style requires greater opacity, you need have no scruple regarding the addition of Zinc White to any colour it is desired to lighten. Zinc White is preferable, since it avoids any unpleasant, chalky effect, and is not so obvious as other whites. If a strong high light is required in some places, use Flake White. For such work use a rough-surfaced canvas. The paints must be mixed much thicker, and so will require a stronger solution of medium to hold them.

Mention has been made of those pigments which need a specially strong medium, and now that thicker colours are to be used, pay special attention to this point. When painting, do not overcharge the brush with colour or the work will dry in patches, while if you proceed to the opposite extreme the painting will have a dry, unpleasant effect.

Architecture, figures and heavy drapery, can be excellently rendered by this manner of painting. Its principal advantages are brilliancy, intensity of colour, and opacity, but there is a corresponding loss in delicacy and softness. The surface can also be very pleasant, provided the opacity is retained uniformly throughout and the flatness not destroyed by a stereoscopic effect.[1] Over-concentration on detail and constant correction should be avoided, for in this case the spoiling of the general effect is even more harmful than with water-colour representation.

In actual practice, it will be found that each sketch requires its own individual technique which lies between the two styles described. Another important point to be considered is the stage lighting required

---

[1] *Pulcinella*, designed by Picasso, is a good example of this style of painting. Buildings, sky and drapery are all painted in colours of the same opacity, adding a pleasant surface to the scene's other qualities.

by the scene. In the majority of cases ordinary white electric light displays the painting to the best advantage, but sometimes the exigencies of the production demand certain changes of lighting, such as the passing from day to night,[1] or permanent special effects, such as moonlight, twilight, and so on.[2] In these cases, bear in mind the most prolonged and important of the lighting schemes. Such difficult problems can only be solved by long experience, instinct and knowledge of the results of stage lighting.

But, while you are considering all these questions, your director is impatient to have his scenery in the theatre. Therefore :—

Fold it with the help of your assistants in the following manner. Take the top edge of the cloth and fold it over the bottom edge so that the two coincide. Grasp the folded edge and again bring it to the bottom.

Repeat this, if necessary. Now bring over to the middle both ends of the folded canvas, so that they do not quite meet. Repeat several times. Now turn one side of the double packet on to the other and the cloth is correctly folded. Write on the bundle the title of the work and description of the cloth (such as back-cloth, cut-cloth, and so on), and, if the master carpenter places it carefully on to its batten in the theatre, after a few hours' suspension, no creases in the canvas will be visible.

Repainting

The repainting of old scenery is a difficult and unpleasant task. Very often the original painting is so obliterated that at first it is quite impossible to make anything of it. Mount the ladder and from this distant point of view it may be possible to make out the scene by a study of what remains of the contour and original masses. Since, in most cases, it is impossible to obtain access to the original designs, prepare your own scheme of colour, and while you are so engaged, instruct your apprentice to take a large, soft brush and glaze the cloth

---

[1] The beautiful Japanese woodcut effect, where day changes into night in *Le Tricorne* designed by Picasso, came unexpectedly, for the colour scheme had been based on white lighting.
[2] The red lighting in *Prince Igor*, designed by Roehrich, is very effective on the panorama of pale, greenish-blue.

with a weaker solution of the medium with which the paints are to be mixed.

Glazing, that is, covering the canvas with a transparent coat, strengthens the old priming, brings out the original colours, and provides a pleasant surface on which to work.

Commence painting, endeavouring to reproduce what you judge to be the characteristics of the original scene. When, fortified with years of practical experience, you are able successfully to combat the damage caused by rainwater, seawater, steam, and so on, the solution of which difficulties we shall consider later, the repainted scene should look like new.[1]

Retouching

In most cases scenery is sufficiently preserved to require only retouching in those parts that are worn or discoloured. Hence, the chief endeavour should be to restore the faded or damaged tones in harmony with the other portions of the scene. If this is well done, the most experienced eye cannot distinguish the newly-painted parts from the old. But, to achieve this result, remember that the former must not appear brighter than the latter.[2]

Stencil

If there is a pattern to be repeated many times, as on curtains, walls, and so on, a stencil must be prepared. Take a piece of Bristol board, draw the design on it and cut out the spaces with a sharp pen-knife, leaving ties. Varnish the back of the stencil thickly with spirit varnish which will prevent the colour running. Take a stencil brush and thickly mixed colour, and stencil the pattern on to the canvas. It is a quick, easy process, but unfortunately tends to give the work a mechanical appearance.

Flats

As flats packed together injure each other through surface friction, the pigments used for painting them should be mixed thickly and with

---

[1] Bakst's *Schéhérazadé, Carnaval,* and *Thamar* ; Benois's *Petrouchka,* and Golovin's *L'Oiseau de Feu*, are examples of scenes completely repainted as new.
[2] Bakst's *Narcisse,* Douboujinsky's *Papillons,* and Delaunay's *Cléopâtre* are examples of scenes that have been retouched.

a stronger solution of medium. Endeavour to simplify the outline of the flats, because profile work is complicated to execute, and tends to be displeasing if over elaborate.

Flats can be painted on canvas nailed to the floor in the usual manner, or previously mounted on their stretchers.

When they are finished, instruct your apprentice to paint the under edges with suitable colour. If stage lights are visible through the flats, either paste paper over the back, or, provided the canvas is sufficiently thick, paint the back, using dry colour.

Properties

Such objects must be well sized before being painted. The pigments should be mixed with a strong solution of medium to prevent their rubbing off and spoiling the costumes of the artistes. Paint the properties in the same style as the scenery, there is no need to finish them more highly simply because they are smaller than their surroundings.

Repairing

A Russian proverb states :—

Cheap, but ever rotten,
Dear, but never forgotten.

Cheap canvas will often be expensive in the long run. Numerous holes, tears and rotten places will be unwelcome visitors in the work of retouching and repainting.

The simplest method of repairing is to turn the cloth face downwards and stick patches over the holes and tears with thick paste and glue. It is quick and answers the purpose, but often the work of repainting will cause the patches to unfasten. Sewing the pieces as a fisherman patches his sails is the best method, but it requires time and skill. The cloth should be laid face upwards and the patches slipped under the holes and sewn with strong thread, using curved needles. Select suitably coloured patches as far as possible, since white canvas is difficult to conceal.

Cleaning

If the surface of the cloth is dull, dusty or mouldy, but does not require repainting, take slightly damped sawdust and sweep it over the surface with a soft broom.   This will brighten and freshen it.

Damage by Rainwater and Seawater

This is a difficult problem. Water dissolves both priming and colour, so that although the offending mark be painted over it will continue to be in evidence although not so pronounced. Many coats of colour must be applied before the mark can be obliterated, and even then, in course of time, it is more than likely to reappear.

Since rainwater soaks through many layers of folded or rolled canvas, it is often necessary to deal with numerous repetitions of the same stain which both takes time and tries one's patience. It has been well said that the inventor of a remedy for stains caused by water will make his fortune.

Seawater is even more dangerous, but this class of damage is less frequent. The affected portion of the scenery never thoroughly dries and on a damp day the enormous marks grow darker.[1]

Steam can also cause troublesome damage.[2]

Preservation, Storage and Transit

Scenery painted by the Continental method can, as we have seen, be easily folded and packed into wooden boxes of medium size. If the boxes are lined with waterproof material the cloths should be safe from rainwater damage. Such boxes are much easier to store and dispatch from one country to another than scenery rolled on tumblers. With reference to flats, which have to travel more or less unprotected, care should be taken not to pack those painted with aniline against those painted with ordinary colours.[3]

[1] Several cloths of Bakst's *Thamar* fell into the sea during shipment, and after being retouched in the studio and drying for over a week had to be sent to the theatre quite wet.
[2] Steam from a swimming bath on the Coliseum stage damaged the back-cloth of Bakst's *Les Femmes de Bonne Humeur* and the aniline of Delaunay's *Cléopâtre*.
[3] The flats of *Pulcinella*, after travelling, developed red stains over the moonlight which constant retouching failed to obliterate.   The cause of this was that the wings of *Thamar*, painted in red aniline, had been packed beside them and, becoming damp through rain, had marked them.

Hanging and Lighting of the Scenery in the Theatre

If the scenery shows unpleasant creases and folds some hours after it has been hung, it is proof that it has not been properly nailed on to the battens, or that the cloths were not properly stretched in the studio. In the first place, insist on the rebattening of the cloth ; in the second, there is no remedy.

Take care not to place the cloth too close to the electric battens, otherwise it is impossible to obtain a uniform lighting over the whole surface. As the lighting depends chiefly on electric battens and foot-lights, only use arc lamps, bunches, and so forth, for gaining an additional effect.[1] Lighting from the dome is sometimes very useful, but, used indiscriminately, becomes vulgar. Again, excess of lighting from the footlights throws the shadows of the performers on to the back-cloth. This must be avoided. Shadows thrown by one cloth on to another can be lessened by counter lighting.

Before commencing the lighting rehearsal, do not forget to make certain that all the auditorium lights are out.

In general, lighting is a difficult matter, requiring taste, experience and knowledge of the lighting possibilities of the theatre in which the production is to be staged, for every theatre has its own peculiarities.

[1] The powerful lighting accommodation recently installed in the London Coliseum in front of the proscenium is an important addition to the lighting facilities.

Section Three

MY WORK FOR SIR THOMAS BEECHAM

HAVING detailed the successive stages in the construction and painting of scenery I feel it necessary to review the soundness of the principles I have evolved from my work of the last ten years. For while the lessons learned will be of great help to the novice, they will be found useful to the experienced scene painter. No work justifies so well the proverb " live and learn," and since scenery is frequently thought out and executed at the last moment of production, all advice is valuable that facilitates the completion of the work to be done.

In 1914, my colleague Boris Anisfeld, an eminent scene painter who has done much to extol the names of Léon Bakst and Alexander Benois, having painted the scenery for *Schéhérazadé* (1st version), *Petrouchka*, and so on, asked me to collaborate with him in his work for Nijinsky who had recently left the Diaghileff Company and was about to open a season on his own account at the Palace Theatre.

The scenery for Nijinsky's productions of *Les Sylphides*, *Le Carnaval*, *Le Spectre de la Rose* and *L'Après-Midi d'un Faune* was painted from Anisfeld's sketches. The business was pressing, since only four weeks could be spared for the work, and it proceeded at the rate of fourteen to sixteen hours daily. I was entrusted with the preparatory labour, *i.e.*, the drawing on the canvas, settling of details and properties, research work in museums, and so forth.

Anisfeld must be regarded as one of the best Russian technicians in scene painting. The scenes painted by him many years ago, such as *Les Préludes*, which he executed for Madame Pavlova, and *Petrouchka* for Diaghileff, have retained their freshness and are without cracks. This may be explained by the thinness of the priming used by him and also by his technique akin to water-colour. During those four weeks of

31

collaboration I acquired the foundation of the theories which are the basis of my present activities. All that I had learned during my residence in Russia did not fit me to carry out a commission single-handed, and it was only the help of Anisfeld that dispelled my dread of working independently on a huge canvas.

In May, 1914, Sir Thomas Beecham commissioned me to design and execute a drop curtain for Mozart's opera *Die Zauberflöte*, and to renovate innumerable scenes of this opera which had been purchased in Germany for his season of German and Russian Opera and Ballet at Drury Lane.

Both tasks proved to be somewhat difficult. The scenes of a poor provincial conception, although technically not indifferently painted, were found to be much too small for the stage at Drury Lane, and moreover did not correspond to the demands of Grand Opera. Each back-cloth had to be enlarged by some 9 feet at both sides, the minute technique of the German decorators had to be simplified, and the construction altered in different places.

The period of two weeks was allotted me for this work, but since, to the best of my memory, the production contained something like fourteen scenes, each of not less than three planes, it will be readily understood that the renovation could not be carried out as completely as might be desired. There were mistakes too. For example, the blue sky in the scene of the Queen of Night began to peel away during the dress rehearsal, so that it had to be glazed with glue water when already at the theatre. Again, the cactuses which formed part of the decorative scheme of one of the scenes appeared so monstrous that, in accordance with Sir Thomas's request, they were painted out on the spot, amid the laughter of the orchestra.

There remained only a week in which to design and execute a huge canvas for the drop curtain, which was stretched on the empty stage of the London Opera House, which Sir Thomas had placed at my disposal. The purpose of this curtain was to unite the mysticism of ancient Egypt with the freemasonry of Mozart's epoch. After hearing the impressive overture to this opera, which was played to me at Sir Thomas's request, I decided to take the scene of the Last Judgment for

my theme.   Osiris and Isis were shown as central figures against a huge
silver sun ; to these I added masonic emblems and framed the whole in
a border based on Egyptian motifs.

The work progressed, with my wife's assistance, literally day and
night, and since, owing to lack of time, the design was not completely
worked out, everything had to be evolved and transferred directly to the
canvas.   There was a large element of risk in proceeding thus on an
immense canvas where the seated figure of Osiris alone measured
15 feet.   There was, however, no alternative, for the curtain had to be
delivered at Drury Lane before the dress rehearsal.

One of the most difficult tasks of a scene painter is the painting of
an act-drop.   There are no planes, no great distances and no effective
forms of lighting ; in short, there are none of those factors which help
and even make a scene.   And though the principle of decorativeness
was applied correctly in this case (*i.e.*, the absence of the lineal perspective, of light and shade, and the " flatness " of the rendering were
felt), it must be admitted that the act-drop for *The Magic Flute*, despite
the happy combination of tones—mauve, silver and grey—is to be
regarded as a graphic work of huge dimensions in which the colours do
not play the chief part.   Many mistakes in technique were made, one
in particular came near to spoiling the whole effect.

The sky, of a delicate mauve, was composed of white, carnation
paste and ultramarine painted in a liquid state upon the whole surface of
the huge canvas.   But to my horror, the sky, instead of being of an
agreeable tone, appeared, when dry, to be covered with reddish-blue
patches with occasional purple blotches.   The cause of this was found
to be due partly to a bad mingling of the red with ultramarine and
partly to the medium employed, in this case French glue.   But it was
mainly the strong fire-proofing of the English canvas, the vagaries of
which were then unknown to me, that produced so indescribable an
effect.   It was found necessary to abandon the water-colour technique
on which the sketch was based, substitute the usual size medium
and paint over the sky with thick colours.

The act-drop was thus rescued but lost considerably in technique
through acquiring the usual whitish tone of native scene painting.   On

33

the other hand, when the system of blue lighting was used at the beginning of the overture to the opera, I succeeded in obtaining a golden effect on the sun and moon, in spite of their having been painted with silver.[1]

In 1915, I designed and executed a huge scene with many planes, for the production of Tschaikovsky's 1812 Overture at the London Coliseum. Although both scenery and costumes received good notices in the Press, the commission had the character of a commercial undertaking appropriate to the demands of war-time. The work proceeded on the empty stage of the London Opera House, to the accompaniment of German air raids, but, although ample time was allowed, mistakes were made in the dimensions. For example, the top and sides were not sufficiently masked in and this had to be corrected at the Coliseum during the night preceding the performance. This was partly due to my mistake in adhering too closely to the producer's desire to secure as much space as possible in order to suggest the vastness of Russia by means of a huge crowd and a wide atmosphere, in paying insufficient attention to the dimensions of the Coliseum stage, and in neglecting the preparation of scale models of the area available.

In 1916, I received another commission from Sir Thomas Beecham to design and paint the scenery for the five acts of Verdi's *Otello* and make sketches for some fifty costumes. I asked Sir Thomas to play through the whole opera for me that I might, in my forthcoming designs, approach as much as possible to the spirit of the music.

Sir Thomas Beecham, with the assistance of Eugene Goossens, played the whole opera and gave his indications regarding the main parts of it. Lady Cunard entered during the performance, and on her asking what was the matter, Sir Thomas replied : " We are playing the scenery for *Otello*." My intention was to render in the designs the fragile sentimentality of Verdi's opera and make the five acts into one decorative whole. Twenty-four large canvases had to be painted, apart from smaller details such as flats, properties, and so forth, and there remained only six weeks to the beginning of the season.

The completion of all this work was rendered possible by Sir

[1] See Carter (Huntly), " The New Spirit in the European Theatre," p. 103.

34

Thomas, who placed at my disposal both the stage and the designer's studio of the Covent Garden Opera House, which enabled four canvases to be worked on simultaneously, so that while one was being primed, another was being drawn, a third painted, a fourth in course of drying, and so on.

The stage at Covent Garden afforded a splendid studio for the painting of scenery. Its huge dimensions, the delightful courtesy of the entire staff, the stage lighting—which enabled one to test the newly painted scene under actual conditions—all helped the work to be well done and completed even before the appointed time.

But, despite such favourable conditions, there were many set-backs. For example, the canvases of the first act were primed much more strongly than was required, so that the general effect was harder than in the scenes for the succeeding acts.

One particularly irritating incident, somewhat similar to that which happened to the drop curtain of *The Magic Flute*, spoilt the effect of the back-cloth used in the second act. Carnation paste mixed with azure blue gave the sky a redder shade than was intended according to the original design, but this time was left unaltered partly through lack of time and partly for fear of spoiling it still more. Strangely enough, many people regarded the effect as a happy one in its unexpectedness. Another mistake occurred in the green carpet of the same act, which faded sooner than was expected owing to the admixture of anilines which always produce a dirty-grey shade.

Again, the draperies, which I intended to paint, were substituted, for lack of time, by others of bought material. In general, purchased materials, even if they are expensive and of good quality, always differ from painted ones, so that it is both better and safer to make and paint such accessories.

In the fourth act of *Otello*, the scene of the reception room, the back-cloth appeared darker than in the design. This was found to be due to its being hung too close to the electric battens, so that the light did not reach its centre and base.

The scene of Desdemona's room in the fourth act, painted with aniline, was free from any untoward incident, with the exception that

35

my wife narrowly escaped the loss of an eye and was unable to work for many weeks. Aniline in grain is dangerous, for one such grain got into her eye, produced severe inflammation and led to serious complications for a considerable period. When working with aniline the greatest care should be taken not to touch the eyes with the hands. But in spite of its disadvantages there are occasions when no substitute can be found for it.

The scenery for *Otello* received enthusiastic notices in all the important newspapers and the public honoured the designer with unanimous and reiterated applause.

Since, owing to war conditions, a proper studio could not be found and the hire of the stage of the London Opera House or Covent Garden Theatre was not always possible apart from the considerable expense, the General Manager proposed that I should adopt the vertical (English) system of painting scenery, with the promise of permanent work for Sir Thomas Beecham. But, as I knew myself unable to express my individuality in such a manner of working, I was obliged to refuse the offer.

From this, or perhaps some other cause, the designs I prepared for *The Magic Flute* were, by request of Sir Thomas, reduced from fourteen scenes to three or four, while my sketches for Rimsky-Korsakoff's *Snegourotchka* were never carried out.

In 1918 Sir Thomas Beecham again approached me regarding scenery for his productions but, being bound by contract to the Diaghileff Company, I was again unable to accept.

Section Four

SEVEN YEARS WITH THE DIAGHILEFF COMPANY

IN August, 1918, I was invited by telegram to meet S. P. Diaghileff. The whole of his company, with bulky scenery, properties and luggage, had just arrived from Paris. At a time when it was difficult to send even a small parcel to Europe, Diaghileff managed to travel with a company of fifty and several railway carriages full of scenery and luggage 40 kilometres away from the firing line. The contract with the London Coliseum was for a season of six weeks, but the company stayed there for many months.

Though I had had no opportunity of making the personal acquaintance of Diaghileff, his many activities in the domain of art were well known to me from former times.

Having entered the artistic world as an organiser of the exhibitions of *Mir Iskousstva*[1] in 1899, Diaghileff, in the course of six years, gave a new direction to the public taste, bringing new life to Russian art. As the director of the magazine mentioned, by means of a series of skilful articles, monographs and reproductions, he overthrew the old gods from their pedestals and set up new ones, whose names were hitherto entirely unknown, but afterwards became of international reputation.

This magazine had for us Russians another important meaning ; it led, for the first time, to our closer acquaintance with the artistic achievements of Europe about which we had desultory notions, often of a negative character. And this bilateral work of his soon placed him in the first rank of cultured workers for the advancement of Russian art. It was his usual practice to visit the studios of those artists whose work interested him, and select, as an omnipotent autocrat, not what

---

[1] *The World of Art.*

the artist wished to be shown, but what he, Diaghileff, considered suitable for a projected exhibition.

A palatial mansion was often taken where everything was kept in a certain style and where the pictures, hung on the walls by a gifted hand, gave a complete impression of harmony in colour. One of these exhibitions was given in the house where Pushkin died. And since the worship of Pushkin and of Old Petersburg inspired many of the contributors to *Mir Iskousstva*, the room, with the inscription : " Pushkin died here," gave the impression of a temple where everybody involuntarily spoke in a whisper. Diaghileff's rare taste, his clear understanding of the purpose and idea of the *ensemble* that penetrated his exhibitions produced an extraordinary result, at that time quite unknown.

But the triumph of his talents as an organiser was the great exhibition of Russian Portrait Painting held in the colossal halls of the Taurida Palace, later to become the seat of the Duma. Diaghileff and his agents travelled for three years over Russia visiting seigniorial halls, public collections and private owners of important portraits. All the portraits comprised in the exhibition were arranged chronologically to illustrate the reigns of the Russian tzars beginning with the first Romanoffs. Each epoch was set in its own *milieu* by the association of emblems, specimens of furniture and other attributes of the period. The impression evoked afforded a wonderful picture of the men, women and styles of bygone times, as the spectator passed from room to room. In the magnitude of the task and the genius displayed in its achievement, nothing in the least approaching it had been attempted before in any country. And, for us Russians, this exhibition had a special significance in that it revealed to us our great masters of portrait painting and the importance of past ages.

In 1906 Diaghileff organised a great exhibition at the Paris Salon which made the French public acquainted with Russian art. This enterprise had a considerable success, and raised Russian art to its rightful eminence in Europe. Before Diaghileff, Paris, the artistic capital, regarded Russian art in the main as imitative. Now, it was impossible for Paris not to recognise the great originality of Russian decorative art.

Seven Years with the Diaghileff Company

When, a few years later, Diaghileff showed his new ballet at Paris, the decorative character of Russian art was at once revealed in all its strength, leaving all European achievements behind. The influence of the triumphs of Russian decorative art, music and choreography is still apparent in many European theatrical productions.

Diaghileff, like a wise ruler, contrived to surround himself with the most eminent artists and became the inspirer of new movements both in art and the world of the theatre. His former collaborators in the *Mir Iskousstva* were closely associated with him in his first theatrical enterprises, for example, Alexander Benois, Bakst, Douboujinsky, Golovin and others, who did so much for the Diaghileff Company and became well known throughout Europe.

Such was Diaghileff with whom I sat one day in August, 1918, in the Savoy Hotel, London, discussing the work of painting the scenery for *Les Femmes de Bonne Humeur*.[1] This had to be executed quickly from a new design by Bakst, since the first conception of this artist had proved so unsuccessful that the ballet was a failure, though, in Diaghileff's opinion, the work would have a great future, being a favourite of his choreographer Leonid Massine.

Without concealing the difficulties of working in wartime, financial troubles, and so on, Diaghileff clearly showed that the success of this ballet would enable his company to rise in every respect to its former eminence. There remained a fortnight to the opening performance, and it was necessary that the painting of the scenery should begin without delay. All the difficulties of finding a studio, procuring canvas and other materials (by no means easy at this period) were quickly surmounted, thanks to Diaghileff's untiring energy and his gift of inspiring all those with whom he came into contact. The studio, at the top of the fruit baskets store at Covent Garden market, at first hired for ten days only, became the repository of Diaghileff's scenery, and there my wife and I worked uninterruptedly for over two years.

To transfer a design by Bakst into suitable proportions for the stage proved to be a difficult task, for he often painted his effective designs with more regard for their pictorial effect than for the use of

---

[1] *The Good-Humoured Ladies.*

39

the scene painter, and so it was in this case. If his design were to be transferred to the prepared canvas in the same proportions, the nearest houses of the back-cloth would have appeared so small that the heads of the dancers would have been on a level with the roofs, which would have destroyed the veracity of the effect. On the other hand, if the buildings were to be of normal size, the top of a tower would have been then cut off by a sky-border.

Diaghileff, who came several times a day to the studio where the work was in progress, immediately decided that the tower should be 27 feet high, and he was right; the sky-border did not spoil the effect and the nobility of the tower gave the proper dimensions to the surrounding buildings. He looked over the details of the drawings, criticised the height of the buildings on both sides of the back-cloth (which were not in the design), chose another type of fountain instead of that depicted by Bakst, which was not to his taste, took an interest in all the details, and did his best to appreciate the point of view of the executors, often agreeing with them.

Another difficulty arose in that Diaghileff's views on the production required that the tone of the sky should be altered; Bakst's " inky " tone, as Diaghileff termed it, was to be changed to a pure Italian blue. Despite my suggestion that an arbitrary change of one of the principal tones might produce a scene inharmonious in colour, he was not to be dissuaded. There was no time to argue, for the work had to be completed, and, in fact, it was accomplished sooner than expected.

Diaghileff then examined the back-cloth with great care, and remarked that the water-colour blotches in Bakst's design had not been reproduced by us. But, on wiping the portions in question with a sponge, we achieved in his presence a perfect imitation of the effect in the design. Diaghileff was so pleased with this process that he always remembered it and requested its application in other cases. The houses at the side, the cut-cloths and other parts did not arouse any objections, and when, at the dress rehearsal, everything was in its right place, Diaghileff said to me : " Thank goodness, at last I have a scene in accordance with what I wanted." Bakst, evidently at Diaghileff's suggestion, sent us a congratulatory telegram on the successful execution of his design.

But this was not the end of our troubles, many were the times we had to return to this scene ; the sky alone had to be repainted eleven times. A few days after the first performance, it was noticed that the sky was dotted with shining grey spots. They were repainted, but reappeared on other portions of the canvas. This phenomenon continued until an act termed *The Diving Nymphs* departed from the Coliseum. A large tank of warm water had been set on the stage, and the rising steam, condensing on the back-cloth, had dissolved the size and brought it to the surface. This cause was not discovered for a long time, so that the enormous surface of the sky had to be repainted nearly every two days. It was only when the scenery for *Cléopâtre*, painted with aniline, which was given alternately with *Les Femmes de Bonne Humeur*, began to show the same symptoms, that the reasons for the change were discovered.

The next year Diaghileff decided to have the sky repainted in accordance with the tone given in Bakst's design. While examining the back-cloth I noticed that it was covered with grains of dissolved glue ; and although these did not visibly affect the earth-coloured houses, they caused the blue sky to show bright lead-coloured patches which had to be removed with great care.

The sky had to be carefully washed off, necessitating much time, patience and scores of pails of hot water. Then the washed surface had to be reprimed and repainted in the tone of the sky in Bakst's design. This had evidently been painted over by Bakst with thick patches of a lighter hue. To paint on the floor with such a technique was difficult, because the final brush marks on the dry background produced an arid effect. I then tried repainting the sky and adding the brush marks while it was still wet, but the walking on a wet background left footprints on the sky. The only course to follow was to paint the background in sections, completing each part as the work progressed. The new sky tone, however, did not meet with Diaghileff's approval when the cloth was hung in the theatre ; he thought that it did not correspond with that in Bakst's design. But, on coming to the studio, he was convinced that the sky was painted in the exact tone of the design, and so the scene remained as it is to-day.

In examining this scene now, after seven years of constant use and without repainting, it must be admitted that it has worn very well. It has no cracks, no partial alterations in tone, only a uniform fading due to the passage of time.

Le Carnaval

On the completion of the scenery for *Les Femmes de Bonne Humeur*, my wife and I came to a yearly agreement with Diaghileff. Nearly all of his scenes were found to be in very bad condition because, owing to wartime, it had been impossible to repair and look after them. There was a great deal of work to be done, such as examining all the scenes, repairing and repainting them, restoring lost parts, and so forth. The repairing and substituting of new material for those pieces of canvas that had become rotten were carried out in one part of the studio, the repainting in another.

The work began with the scene for *Le Carnaval*, which was given after *Les Femmes de Bonne Humeur*. Each time that a scene had to be renovated, Diaghileff gave his instructions regarding the repainting and the former aspect of it. He had not retained the original designs for his scenes, so that all his instructions were most important, especially as some parts of the scenes were so damaged that it was extremely difficult to make out what they had been like.

The scene for *Le Carnaval* was so worn that it was reduced to a sieve. The priming had gone, and the colour at the slightest brushing flew off or fell through the canvas to the floor. There was no time left for priming, everything had to be repainted as it stood. And if one considers that this scene was painted with ivory black at the top and ultramarine at the base, colours notoriously lacking in adhesive qualities, it will be readily understood that they rubbed off at the slightest touch, soiling the costumes of the dancers.

But though the repainted scene succeeded better than the old one, the constant peeling away of the colours and the damage done to the costumes afforded a continual source of anxiety. In addition, owing to the lack of priming and the presence of a thick fire-proof fluid, it was found that the colour powder was in excess to the proportion of size used. This resulted in a very brilliant but technically unsatisfactory tone. But Diaghileff said: " Let it rub off, it is better than size glittering on it."

In further connection with this scene it was found that a mixture of gold and gelatine, often used successfully in Russia, became instantly black when dry, and lost its bright effect. Hence another vehicle had to be tried. This was gold size, less elastic, and producing a hard outline, but which was less affected by fire-proof fluid. This scene was afterwards repainted many times, so long as the worn canvas would permit of it. Later it was replaced by a duplicate (not executed by us), which, however, possessed the same negative properties.

Schéhérazadé

Schéhérazadé, a scene of huge dimensions, had been painted by Charbet from a design (2nd version) by Bakst; the original scene, painted by Anisfeld, having worn out long ago.

As usual, attention had to be concentrated on the back-cloth. In general, blue tones painted with ultramarine become damaged more quickly than any others. Ultramarine either peels away, if the quantity of size used has been insufficient, or blackens so that the tone resembles some dirty reddish-purple mass. At first glance, it is difficult to ascertain what colours have been used, for only after the closest investigation can one be certain that it is ultramarine and then decide whether it is the light or deep variety. As this colour figured prominently in Bakst's scenes, and was often used in them for the outlines of adjacent surfaces and for shadows, it became sufficient in many cases to renew the ultramarine, when the scene at once acquired a fresh and clear appearance.

One of the present problems was to renovate the scene for *Schéhérazadé*, which had sunk in considerably and was damaged, find again its former bright fundamental tones and bind them with the innumerable details of pattern so characteristic of Bakst's work. Diaghileff insisted not only that the correct harmony of the tones—the blue of the ceiling, the emerald green of the walls, and the pink of the curtain—should be obtained, but also the imperceptible blending of light and shade in Bakst's design by which he suggested the character of the materials of which the scene was supposed to consist ; that is to say, the colossal drapery, with its many planes, must appear to be silk ; the walls, polished stone, and so forth. Having no sketch for guidance, but only separate portions of a half-faded scene, we were forced to proceed very carefully, almost to grope for the tones, so that the sonorous harmony of the whole might be attained.

Although the painting of the back-cloth was technically rather easy, the drapery, consisting of two cut-cloths and many wings, offered considerable difficulty. The rendering of folds is always difficult, but when these are decorated with intricate patterns, it requires much time, skill and patience to ensure that the tones shall be in their respective places and blend with the folds. And when it is remembered that a vari-coloured pattern in blue, green, pink and gold is repeated over every square yard of this portion of the scene, it will be easy to realise the number of tones and caprices of drawing with which one had to contend.

In this scene, the stage cloth, consisting of a complicated pattern on a vermilion ground, is of great importance, and required much time. It necessitated the use of thick paint which, as a rule, adheres badly to unprimed canvas ; for a carpet cannot be primed, since it loses its softness and elasticity, which prevent its being properly stretched on the stage.

The central doors on the flats, the Shah's throne and the columns, having been left on the Continent on account of their bulk, had to be reconstructed and painted. The throne and columns were carried out in accordance with designs prepared by me after visiting the British Museum with Diaghileff. Now new parts, even when introduced into a scene freshly repainted, invariably detract from the whole, because the colours on a new canvas appear so much brighter. Therefore complete harmony could be obtained only by painting them in a lower key.

Diaghileff entered whole-heartedly into the smallest details, trying to remember the effect of the original scene. Assisted by my wife, he

PLATE II

DESIGN BY VLADIMIR POLUNIN FOR
DROP CURTAIN OF *SHIP AHOY!*

chose bright satins to be appliquéed on to the cushions and the canopy above the throne, asked our advice how to employ them, and in general displayed a wonderful energy and enthusiasm, which he communicated to everybody. When all was complete, he said : " Now I shall have a *Schéhérazadé* the like of which never has been seen anywhere." The general effect of the scene was altogether satisfactory. It was free from errors in techinque, and so well lighted by Diaghileff at the Coliseum, that no single performance of this ballet as given later at the Grand Opera, Paris, or at Monte Carlo, could be compared with it.

However, Diaghileff was of the opinion that the general tone of the scene was slightly deeper than that of the original version. This was true, because the emerald green tone pervading the whole had not been painted with permanent green which, owing to war time, was of such poor quality that we used instead the expensive, beautiful, but slightly bluish, viridian. But perhaps that was the reason why the lighting of the London performance was so successful.

When *Schéhérazadé* was given in Paris a few years later, the scene had to be repainted. This we did from the original designs by Bakst preserved in the section of the Louvre devoted to Decorative Art. The raw and slightly vulgar emerald-green tone of the sketch was reproduced in the scene but, despite its brightness and depth, the introduction of the original throne—the female figures of which had been painted personally by Bakst—and some added columns, the impression was far removed from that attained by the repainted scene used previously in London.

Recalling the effect produced by the original scene painted by Anisfeld, it must be admitted that Bakst found in him an eminent interpreter of his ideas, for one marvels how it was possible to evolve from such a design a scene which gave a new direction to European taste and established a standard which has persisted to the present day.

Papillons

The repainting of the setting for *Papillons* presented few difficulties, apart from the painting of a new pavilion which had to correspond with the general effect of the scene. Only a few portions of the back-cloth were repainted, partly owing to its good state of preservation, and partly because Diaghileff did not attach any importance to this ballet.

It is of interest to note that the scene painter, at the first execution of this scene, had made a technical error, the effect of which was felt whenever the ballet was given ; for the cut-cloth always produced unpleasant folds, and the wings were never straight. This complicated the hanging of the scene and gave rise to constant reproofs from Diaghileff who was always very particular that scenes should be properly set.

While the parts in question were being repainted, it was discovered that the legs of the cut-cloths were of different widths and the wings were not straight. Evidently, when the canvas had been stretched for painting, insufficient attention had been paid to this important operation. Probably, the canvas had been removed from the floor while still damp so that, not being secured by nails, it had shrunk in drying. This apparently insignificant error led to constant correction to the very rise of the curtain. To overcome this defect, it was necessary to examine and check all the canvases, cut them to their correct measurements, and repaint the architectural portions in accordance with the new dimensions.

Les Sylphides

We had to convert a scene for *Las Meninas*, designed by Socrate, into a setting for *Les Sylphides*. It represented a park, which was depicted in the reddish-brown tone of an engraving, and consisted of two planes only. Now, a scene in three planes was required.

At this time Diaghileff, otherwise occupied, seldom visited the studio, leaving to us complete liberty of action. Having altered the composition in many places, with the exception of the centre portion (the pond and the balustrade) we decided to take viridian as a fundamental tone since, in our opinion, this colour combined with green lighting would produce an effective result.

The first cut-cloth had to be drawn and painted in accordance with the style of the converted scene but, as the acquisition of new canvas was at this time not to be considered, various fragments of old ballet scenes had to be sewn together for the work. In one corner of the studio was piled a collection of old canvases (the scenes for *Le Dieu Bleu*, *L'Après-Midi d'un Faune*, and other ballets), which awaited their turn to be used in such cases.

At the lighting of the transformed scene for *Les Sylphides*, Diaghileff remarked laughingly : " Why, that is not Socrate, it is Polunin." And if I remember aright, this ballet was and still is given without any mention being made as to the name of the designer responsible for the scene. In course of time this scene, owing to damage resulting from rain and transport, has been repainted several times because of the reappearance of the reddish tones of the former *Las Meninas*, which had to be obliterated constantly with green.

Contes Russes

Fourteen important pieces of the scenery for *Contes Russes*[1] were burned in a train when the company was touring in America. These had to be replaced, and all three acts of this ballet set in order. Diaghileff decided to abolish the fourth act and have a new act-drop painted for the episode of the Swan Princess. He asked me to design this new scene but, as the entire scenery for this ballet had been painted from the designs by Larionoff, I suggested that it would be preferable to ask him to make a new drawing and so avoid breaking the continuity of impression. It was finally arranged that I should paint from a design by Larionoff provided it arrived in time from Paris, failing which I was to use my own. Larionoff's sketch came to hand on the last day of the term fixed.

This new scene had to be painted on the reverse side of the back-cloth for the fourth act, but, owing to this having been painted with aniline, reddish tints appeared on the water and white lilies of the newly-painted drop curtain. Though these portions have been repainted many times, and even covered with shellac, the reddish tint continues to reappear.

Stout thread not being available at this time, everything had to be sewn with ordinary cotton, which was not nearly strong enough for heavy canvas. Once, during the performance of this scene, the curtain

---

[1] *Children's Tales.*

47

caught on a wing, split up, and fell in two pieces. Hence it is most important that the ends of the seams should be fastened off securely in order to strengthen the weaker parts as much as possible.

All the flats, the rostrum, dragon, horse, three pairs of wings, two borders, one cut-cloth, and so on, were painted on old canvases which formerly had been partly painted with aniline, which is always injurious to painting. For example, the white horse had to be repainted many times because the green aniline of the scene for *L'Après-Midi d'un Faune* was always working through.

Diaghileff decided to have the scene for the third act painted in green, remarking : " I want it to be spring-like, instead of looking like a banana forest." And the scene took on the aspect of spring much to the displeasure of the designer (as I learned later). But Diaghileff persuaded him that, owing to the difficulty of procuring ochre in London in war time (!), green tones had perforce to be used. As a rule, Diaghileff repeatedly altered the ideas of the designer, and though this somehow destroyed the unity of the original, it was, on the other hand, justified by the actual demands of the production.

An interesting incident occurred in connection with this scene. When lighting this production, Diaghileff asserted that the back-cloth had been hung upside down, despite the assurances of Grigorieff, his stage-manager, to the contrary. For myself, I could not express an opinion in favour of either, partly because the top was not marked on the cloth, partly because the design, owing to its composition, lost nothing even when hung upside down. This misunderstanding was not explained until the day following when, owing to the chance discovery by Grigorieff of a reproduction of the design in an old programme, the hanging of the scene, to Diaghileff's astonishment, was found to be correct.

The back-cloth for the second act, which consisted of an enormous red sky, required to be carefully repainted, but at this time it was quite impossible to obtain the requisite large quantity of vermilion, and the following dialogue ensued :—

POLUNIN. It is impossible to find any vermilion, and the other red tones available are all very bad.

48

DIAGHILEFF. There is no interest in achieving the possible, but it is exceedingly interesting to perform the impossible.

POLUNIN. How can that be ?

DIAGHILEFF. Did you think it was possible in war time for me to come to London with my company and remain here for six months instead of a few weeks ? The impossible became possible. I am not interested in what is available or what is not, all I know is that the work must be done.

And since, after a careful examination, it was clear that the sky had to be painted over with finely-ground vermilion, if only in the more damaged parts, the impossible was performed—but at what cost ! In time I became aware that neither price nor difficulty could prevent Diaghileff from carrying out matters which he regarded as important. In general, the scenery for *Contes Russes* produced the effect of a complete whole, as the ballet is given at the present day.

Thamar

The case containing the scenery for *Thamar* had fallen into the sea during one of the voyages of the company. And when the scenes were unfolded in the studio they not only proved to be damp, but the whole area of the back-cloth and a part of the cut-cloth were seen to be covered with enormous spots from two to three yards in diameter.

The brine had evidently been allowed to exert its corrosive action for a considerable period, and it was difficult to determine how the damage could be repaired. The scene could not be washed in the flowing waters of the Thames, as a chemical expert had advised in jest, so it was decided first to dry the scenes in the studio and then repaint them in the usual manner, in the hope that the result might be successful.

The scene for *Thamar*, like nearly all the settings designed by Bakst, consisted of minutely patterned cloths which added considerably to the difficulty of removing the blemishes mentioned. All the tones had to be renewed step by step, irrespective of their durability. Despite the lapse of time, the canvas would not dry, and a repainted wing lay six days as wet as when first painted ; and in this condition the scene had to be dispatched to the theatre. But, to the surprise of everyone, the colours adhered firmly, and this scene has retained its proper appearance, although a certain dampness persists.

When *Thamar* was lighted, the reflection from a fire-place reached the silver setting of an ikon, producing a beautiful effect which caused Diaghileff to remark that what Bakst had sought for so long had at last been found. This result was produced accidentally, through the wings of the fireplace being set at a more acute angle than formerly, so that the artificial glow from the fire reached the back-cloth.

Sadko

The intricate scenes designed and executed by Anisfeld for this ballet were largely mounted on net. These, too, had been injured by water and had become stuck to one another. But the fine technical quality of this artist's painting enabled the scenes to be saved in many places, whereas had they been painted in a thick technique as in the case of *Contes Russes*, they would have had to be condemned.

In this case the principal work consisted in separating the parts which adhered together, repairing the torn canvas and net, and restoring the gold and silver which invariably disappear in the course of time. With the exception of ultramarine, all the colours were in a good state of preservation and sufficiently fresh in appearance.

As a rule, practice proves that scenes painted thinly with high-grade colours and good medium last a long time. Again, if the colours fade, the change extends uniformly over the canvas without affecting the harmony of the whole, as in pictures by the old masters. On the other hand, scenes painted thickly, such as those for *Soleil de Nuit* and *Contes Russes*, despite their apparent brightness, peel away (often right down to the priming), fade in patches, and spoil the general impression, necessitating a constant repainting of the whole scene, which consequently adds greatly to the original cost.

Prince Igor

Through lack of space and time, the colossal panorama for *Prince Igor* was only partly retouched, although repainted later by one of my pupils under the personal direction of the designer, Roehrich.

First, owing to the loss of the wings representing columns of smoke, these had to be reconstructed and painted ; while six tents, also in bad condition, had to be put in order. The tents had to be repainted many times, for the colours peeled away because the canvas had never been primed, or only slightly so.

Here again is an example of how a mistake made at the beginning can be the source of continual anxiety and loss of time and money. In general, whenever I suspected defective priming, I reprimed the whole, time permitting, before beginning the work of restoration. This was the only way to fix the colours permanently, but it was not always possible, because the process of repriming alters the tones to such an extent that it may be difficult to renew them from memory. Glue water, though without effect on the tones, does not always prove sufficiently binding. As regards flats, which suffer particularly during transport, it is generally advisable to prime them heavily and paint them with an extra strong medium, thus avoiding trouble, layers of many colours, and the consequent expense and loss of time.

L'Oiseau de Feu

The scene for *L'Oiseau de Feu* [1] is one of the largest used by the Diaghileff Company. It is painted in an original technique of separate brush-marks akin to pastel. Viewed both from a technical and artistic standpoint, it was interestingly painted by Sapounoff (a young artist now deceased) and Charbet, from a design by Golovin. Though the scene had faded somewhat at the time it came into our hands, the harmony of the tones, the sense of completeness and the originality of construction made the task of repairing a pleasant one.

Diaghileff requested me to retain the Gobelin character of the scene which necessitated the careful blending of innumerable tones and the painting, stroke by stroke, of every part of it in order to recapture the former delicate harmony of the whole.

Since this scene had originally been well painted technically, the renewal of the tones proceeded without any set-backs. In fact, the work resembled the delicate process of restoration rather than the usual

[1] *The Fire-Bird.*

alteration and refreshing of tones. If the technique of the painting of the scene, with its minute and numerous colours, be compared to mosaic, the reader will be better able to appreciate the time and labour expended in the task. This, however, had its reward in the interest afforded by such an experiment and by the achievement of a successful result. Later, in Paris, I repainted the scene in all its details in a slightly heightened key.

Narcisse

The scene for *Narcisse*, painted many years ago, was in such an excellent condition that only certain colours, ultramarine and various green tones, required to be renewed. A splendid Russian canvas of delicate and stout texture, which seemed as good as new, a thin but adequate priming, a water-colour technique, intense colouring, required little attention to produce the impression that the scene had only just been painted. The flats, however, were badly damaged and torn, while the colours were rubbed away and wanting in some places. To put them in order required more time and labour than the restoration of the huge back-cloth.

When Diaghileff saw the scene at the dress rehearsal, he thought that the colours of the back-cloth were not strong enough, and requested me to repaint it, though the first performance had been announced for the following day. I had only three hours at my disposal, but in this short space of time I managed to repaint successfully the back-cloth, which measured 55 × 35 feet. Sometimes, lack of time leads to happy results, for when there is no opportunity to ponder over and correct one's work the scene retains its freshness.

When, some years later, the scenery for *Narcisse* was examined at Monte Carlo, it was found to be in excellent condition and though still in use has not needed any restoration. This scene is one of the best examples of the use throughout of a correct technique, the benefits of which will be appreciated so long as the scene lasts.

Soleil de Nuit[1]

This very simple scene had been damaged by water. The colours had peeled away considerably, due to the use of concentrated pigment

[1] *The Midnight Sun.*

and insufficiently strong medium. The spots caused by water gave a great deal of trouble, as they had several times to be painted, dried and repainted. Only then was it possible to retouch the whole surface and repaint it completely. The result was not successful, as in time the water spots reappeared, necessitating further restoration and complete repainting. Hence the back-cloth has to be continually examined and put in order as occasion arises.

Le Tricorne

One day, while the work of restoration, repainting and renewing the former scene was in progress, Diaghileff came into the studio accompanied by a gentleman of medium height, southern complexion and wonderful eyes, whom he introduced to me as Pablo Picasso. After mutual greetings, Picasso showed me the booklet-*maquette* of his scene for a new ballet *Le Tricorne*,[1] and we all began discussing the construction of the future setting. Having dealt so long with Bakst's complicated and ostentatious scenery, the austere simplicity of Picasso's drawing, with its total absence of unnecessary detail, the composition and unity of the colouring—in short, the synthetical character of the whole—was astounding. It was just as if one had spent a long time in a hot room and then passed into the fresh air.

The next day I planned out the constructional model according to Picasso's booklet, and the nobility of the tones, the harmony of the composition, the voluntary divergence from the laws of perspective produced an artistic whole even with the absence of colour. Both Diaghileff and Picasso approved my model without any alteration, and the work proceeded in a spirit of exultation.

Picasso came to the studio daily, evinced a keen interest in everything, gave his instructions regarding the drawing and requested us to preserve its individuality and pay special attention to the colouring. The drawing, despite its deviation from the usual perspective, was set down with mathematical precision. The tones, of which there were four fundamental ones, were reproduced to a high degree of exactitude.

---

[1] *The Three-Cornered Hat.*

All this care was of the utmost importance, for the entire scene was based on the very clever combination of the four fundamental tones and on a deeply meditated composition. The colours appeared remarkably quiet and required the addition of zinc white, a proceeding which, in scenes of the Bakst type, would have been considered a crime ; but Picasso maintained that this led to a general unity of tone and effected a uniform opacity of colour.

In general, Picasso's theories were diametrically opposed to those held by the majority of Russian scene painters. The latter employed both thick and thin colours on the same canvas as the need arose, considering the admixture of white with all tones inadmissible since, in their opinion, it destroyed the brilliancy of the colours. The brightness of the ultramarine in Picasso's sky was dulled by the addition of a combination of zinc white with a certain amount of ivory black. The force of the ivory black of the doors, houses, and so on, was neutralised by the admixture of zinc white and burnt sienna. The latter colour, combined sometimes with zinc white and sometimes with ivory black, produced soft and unexpected combinations. The pure white was dulled by the addition of light chrome, which resulted in a tone having the beauty of old ivory. Picasso was invariably present at these experiments and though often accepting our advice, never departed in the slightest degree from the colour-key and construction he had evolved. His presence during the execution of the work gave a special charm to the joint solution of all questions.

With him, there were never any of the doubts, alterations and variations so characteristic of " designers " of inferior calibre, which react against the successful execution of a scene. Different proposals and variations were discussed while deciding on the colours, but, once everything had been settled, the given tone was not altered on the canvas by a hair's breadth. For example, when the tone of the walls, which comprise nearly a third of the scene, could not be obtained after many experiments, so that Picasso was half inclined to accept pure white without any admixture, he instantly agreed with our suggestion that it might alter the combination of tones and the delicate shade of the walls in his sketch. And when at last a combination of zinc white with

DESIGN BY PABLO PICASSO
FOR *LE TRICORNE*

PLATE 12

light chrome gave the desired effect (neither ochre nor sienna gave the correct result) he passed it immediately without question.

The justness of his decision was brought home to me many years later when, on examining the canvas, I noticed that the flats representing the walls had at some time been repainted with pure white which had destroyed the meaning and beauty of the delicate colouring. The canvas, as originally executed by us, was primed very thinly, since it was desired to render the soft silkiness pervading the surface of Picasso's sketch.

He did not introduce light and shade into his design, and had no recourse to garish contrasts of the Bakst type, but built everything on the precision of calm tones, so that great care had to be exercised both in the drawing and the colours, and due attention paid to the *matière* of the painting. This scene was painted with broad parallel sweeps of the brush, using not thick, but rather opaque colours. A slightly noticeable roughness of the brush marks on the sky was well contrasted with the flatter tones of the ivory-hued walls and the reddish and grey tones of the houses. The flats were painted in the same opaque colours, so that the *matière* of the scene, which played so important a part in this case, should remain unaltered.

Diaghileff laughingly transmitted to me Picasso's wish to paint the stars on the sky with his own hand, which he informed me he had granted on the strict condition that no blot should be made. Picasso, putting on slippers, then painted on the back-cloth seven stars and the silhouette of the distant town.

The drop-curtain having been drawn and the general tones carefully roughed in, Picasso himself set to work on its central portion while my wife and I prepared the colours and helped him in everything. After working on the curtain for more than a fortnight, he asked me to stop him when, according to the demands of the stage (which he said I knew better than he did), he had achieved the most suitable result. This I did. Diaghileff expressed his admiration to Picasso, embracing him, and thanked us for the execution of the scene.

Although this scene had been planned in accordance with the usual lighting, the changes expressive of the passing from day to night, and night to dawn, introduced by Diaghileff, proved to be exceedingly interesting. The scene, owing to the presence of some soft reddish tints, acquired the aspect of a Japanese print which, so far from impairing its beauty, endowed it with a certain unexpected charm.

From the technical standpoint, the scene proved to be well painted and, though in constant use, was not renovated for six years. Only at a still later date, when badly damaged by rain, was it retouched with thick paint by somebody and so lost its silkiness. And since the secret of the tone of the houses was not known to the scene-painter responsible, the beauty of the ivory shade had departed, the scene had become faded and lost its charm. However it remains to the present day one of the most interesting scenes of the Diaghileff Company.

La Boutique Fantasque [1]

While we were meditating the execution of a new ballet scene from a sketch by Sert and had actually begun to paint the back-cloth for *The Gardens of Aranjuez*, Diaghileff entered the studio and requested us to stop work and wash out what had been done, saying that the setting for *La Boutique Fantasque*, a ballet long ago projected, was to be painted instead and begun immediately.

Knowing that Bakst had long ago been engaged in preparing designs for this ballet, and was daily expected to arrive in London, we were greatly surprised to learn from Diaghileff that he had been unable to come to terms with him, and hence the sketches would be designed by the " young " French artist, A. Derain.

A few days later, I made his acquaintance on the stage of the Alhambra Theatre, where the company was then performing. Derain was a man of colossal stature, calm aspect, and endowed with a strong will. His design, painted in oils, at first glance seemed to me so untheatrical that I could hardly conceive how it might be used for the stage. Diaghileff, too, seemed to have some doubts, so that a certain perceptible mutual uneasiness existed between the designer and executor at the very outset, which did not seem to promise satisfactory results. But later on, when Derain himself began to take an active part in the

[1] *The Fantastic Shop.*

work, often diverging from or rather developing the ideas contained in his rough design as he proceeded, everything fell into its right place.

The design was so faintly felt that it was difficult even to guess at Derain's ideas. The back-cloth behind the walls and windows could hardly be understood, and I had to ask Derain to make a separate drawing of this portion as he desired it to be ; this he did the next day, in pen and ink. The tones, often very different from those in the original design, were at once prepared and transferred to the canvas. At first, Derain, who alone understood the purposes contained in his design, did not follow anyone's advice, but Diaghileff requested me to alter the general tone of the walls, painted with burnt sienna, to a quiet pinkish-brown. Hence I saw myself drawn two ways, and wondered in which direction lay the artistic truth. This state of affairs continued until Diaghileff and Derain came to an understanding, when the designer and ourselves were left to our own devices.

The chief difficulty in planning the scene arose from the fact that the back-cloth was not sufficiently visible through the enormous windows. The latter, however, could only be enlarged up to a certain degree of stage possibility. Again, Massine's choreography, which always required the maximum of stage space, led to a certain emptiness in the setting of the scenery. Hence we had to effect a compromise in both cases until an acceptable disposition of the scene, according to the constructional model, became possible.

Derain paid little attention to the accurate rendering of drawing and tones ; for example, when, without consulting him, all the houses had been painted slightly cream instead of white, he did not express his displeasure, but on the contrary considered this tone better than that in the original design. Often altering and introducing new details, he paid no heed to warnings of a technical character, but used such thick colours that he ran the risk of their cracking and peeling off ; in fact, this actually occurred in the case of the fruit painted by him into the foliage of some bushes. The flowers at the right window he purposely altered, while those on the other side were left as I had painted them.

In general, he appeared to ignore all the demands of technique and stage requirements, proceeding in an elementary manner known only to himself. The addition of curtains to the windows and entrance gates, required by the action of the ballet, were reluctantly conceded by him. The pieces of furniture were painted straight on to the walls of the " *boutique*," but their perspective did not correspond with the normal perspective employed in the general scene. However, despite these variations, the final result was of great consequence, and *La Boutique Fantasque* which, as Diaghileff declared in his speech at the dress rehearsal at the Alhambra, was more like a restaurant on the Lake of Geneva than a fantastic shop, became the favourite ballet of the London public.

Costumes, curtains, properties, scenery, all seemed out of key with the general idea of the ballet, but in spite of that what a good laugh we had to the accompaniment of the lively airs gleaned from Rossini's note-books. Particularly humorous in a childlike way was the drop-curtain on which Derain had painted two figures and a hill with a three-cornered hat on it. This afforded an excellent accompaniment to the playful overture of the ballet, and I remember how Diaghileff, Derain, Picasso and other visitors, looking at the curtain before it was dispatched to the theatre, could not refrain from a smile at the sight of those incoherent figures, double basses, palm trees and flying birds. The gay spirit of both scene and ballet justified itselves and the designer and painters were rewarded by the great success achieved by the production.

With the exception of the slight technical deficiencies mentioned, no others occurred, and this scene, painted in 1919, has never been repainted, and even at the present time is in good condition. In this, as in Picasso's *Le Tricorne*, each tone was slightly dulled with zinc white and, though there are no strong contrasts and vivid tones, this scene is no less bright and effective than any of the brilliant and some-what pretentious conceptions of Bakst.

In course of time, French painters have learned how to achieve brightness of impression by linking together simple tones—terre verte, sienna, ivory black, ultramarine, and so forth—to which a slight pro-portion of zinc white has been added. And so painters of easel pictures were brought into the service of theatrical art without any sacrifice or concession on either side.

Parade

As Picasso remained some weeks in London during the work on *La Boutique Fantasque*, Diaghileff asked me to revise *Parade* in the designer's presence. The impressive drop-curtain for this ballet did not require repainting, with the exception of a few details ; on the other hand, the scene needed serious attention. Picasso complained that the latter, hurriedly painted by someone in Paris, was so unsatisfactory that it required to be repainted before almost every performance. The black tones so injured the white, and *vice versâ* that, instead of clearly-defined black and white surfaces, there remained only patches of nondescript colour.

On examination of the canvas it was found that the priming had been applied carelessly so that the colours peeled off, hence it was not surprising that when the scenes were folded the tones printed off on each other. The process of continual repainting was no remedy, for there was nothing on the canvas to cause the newly-applied colours to adhere. However, as the combination of black, white and pinkish tones, and the drawing, were of the simplest, it was possible to reprime the whole cloth after having first removed all loose colours. When the canvas was thoroughly dry, all the parts were repainted with so satisfactory a result that no retouching has since been necessary. The result of the mistakes made in the original painting of this scene shows how careless initial work can affect a canvas during the whole period of its existence.

Unfortunately, it is practically impossible to reprime completely scenes having a complicated colour scheme, when the original sketch is not available, because the new strong priming dulls the existing tones to such an extent that it is a matter of extreme difficulty to restore them afterwards from memory.

Petrouchka

The scene for *Petrouchka*, technically very well painted by Anisfeld from sketches by Alexander Benois, would not have required repainting if rain had not spotted the whole sky of the back-cloth and the borders, and the ultramarine on the second proscenium (the first

59

Murrell Library
Missouri Valley College
Marshall, Missouri 65340

proscenium was missing) drop-curtain and flats had not faded as usual. Since it was impossible to paint out the innumerable stains, the whole of the back-cloth had to be painted with a transparent coat which, though it did not completely hide the blemishes, served to soften them and give the impression of the vibrations in a Russian sky in winter. The drop-curtain which depicted an enormous figure of a magician seated on clouds (the face of which was painted by the eminent artist, Seroff), offered an excellent example of Benois's style, and had to be repainted very carefully in the manner and technique of the designer.

I renewed the lost proscenium from a photograph and by questioning those who remembered its original tones. Of the Moor's room, only one wall remained and so another had to be painted on new canvas ; it was no easy task to unite the new and the old colouring with its intricate distribution of tones. The repainting of Petrouchka's black room, the colour of which had rubbed off considerably, led to its being reprimed, while the magician's portrait, which had been executed in a surprisingly ignorant and unskilful manner, was repainted. This portrait, according to Diaghileff, had been wonderfully painted some time ago by Seroff also ; but afterwards, owing to a misunderstanding, it had been retouched, to the horror of everyone, by Diaghileff's co-director, Baron Gunzbourg, who had a passion for visiting the scene-painting studio and repainting everything that happened to be near at hand. In this way he " improved " on Seroff's work, which evidently had not met with his approval. Diaghileff held in high esteem everything painted by Seroff and, on my asking him why he did not use the drop-curtain painted by this artist for *Schéhérazadé*, he replied : " Why drag it about ? It has an enormous value."

It was only the flats of *Petrouchka* which, owing to their being constantly travelled and restored, were in bad condition and required partial repainting. When watching a performance of this ballet as a member of the audience, a practice I adopted in order to verify my work, I expressed to Diaghileff my opinion that the appearance of Petrouchka's ghost at the end was the climax of the ballet. In reply to this, Diaghileff told me an interesting story. When the dress rehearsal of this ballet—which originally ended with Petrouchka's death—was given many years ago, Diaghileff declared that something was lacking, that he felt the end was not complete and therefore refused to give the ballet the next day.

Neither Benois nor Stravinsky, the composer of the wonderful music for the ballet, would consent to any alteration, saying that his work was complete, but Diaghileff would not give way. And presently, at his suggestion, a different ending was substituted, new music added and the ballet performed as it is still given, evoking always the greatest enthusiasm. Here again, Diaghileff is seen as the dominant personality of the company, the members of which hold the unanimous opinion that, deprived of his leadership, it would cease to exist.

Le Chant Du Rossignol

Matisse, the designer of the scenery for *Le Chant du Rossignol*, arrived from France without any sketches or definite plans. After having visited with me different museums, he set to work in the studio, scissors in hand, cutting out and piecing together a model. This work took a fortnight. His complete ignorance of the stage was surprising, so that the very alphabet of it had to be explained to him. Being a man of strong character, he often tried to discover his own America, only to return painfully and unwillingly to the one already known.

Changes of plan, alternating periods of depression and exultation, accompanied the minute work on his model the whole time it was in preparation and, despite his being an eminent painter of easel pictures, his lack of knowledge of the stage was made manifest in a very short time. His model was of a very simple, almost austere character, and its concentrated tones, well combined and balanced, produced at once a soft and brilliant impression, free from any garish contrasts. He left me to paint the scene and departed for Paris, saying that I should do it much better in his absence. The scene, which suggested a Chinese porcelain mannikin, was successful.

Working from a coloured model, instead of from a design, is difficult and rarely productive of a good result. In the first place, the model has to be taken to pieces in order to see the colours on the same plane as the cloth and not as when placed at different angles in a model.

Again, the shadows of the model do not correspond in their dimensions with those of the stage owing to the complexity of stage lighting.

Secondly, the distances between the planes on the model and those on the stage produce combinations of tone differing from those on the flat plane of a sketch or canvas ; in short, a built coloured model cannot correspond to a design where the colours are all on one plane. Hence, in a model, it is possible to obtain the general impression of the tones only and not their actual combination.

However, in spite of the many difficulties, I managed to reproduce the general impression of the scene, as in the end Matisse had instinctively realised in his model the decorative principles of the art of the theatre. But having to proceed carefully, almost gropingly, it was far from easy to reproduce the effect ; whereas a design, in which everything is explained on a flat surface, would have obviated such difficulties. For this reason, Russian painters never use coloured models, but sometimes employ plain ones to solve problems of construction, when these are likely to be complicated, and for working out the details of masking in. And since colour is the basis of all Russian scenery, a sketch was, and continues to be, with Russian artists the starting point of their work.

The decision to have a drop-curtain necessitated Matisse's return to London, but again he brought no sketches, with the exception of one in pencil, so that the tones had to be composed on the canvas. Having begun with the lion on the left, he presently gave it up as he thought that the one on the right, painted by me, was more successful. *Le Chant du Rossignol* did not become popular for many reasons and Matisse did not return to this branch of art, evidently recalling his own words : " Oh ! how difficult it is to work for the theatre ! "

Returning to a *technical* consideration of this scene, it cannot be gainsaid that the result was poor, but the question of how to avoid such a catastrophe in the future has still to be solved. It was noticed during the progress of the work that the canvas dried slowly and that the colours did not adhere to it. On examining the cloth, it appeared that the fire-proof fluid was so strong that it had destroyed the adhesive qualities of the medium, leaving the pigments loose on the canvas so that they rubbed off to a considerable extent.

While the scenery was being taken across the Channel, the vessel in which it was shipped was caught in a squall, with the result that the cases containing the scenes were soaked in rain and brine so that the damaged parts had to be repainted on arrival in Paris. The decorator who repainted these scenes at the Grand Opera evidently employed a different medium which destroyed the suggestion of Chinese porcelain without remedying the peeling away of the colours. Here were displayed all the difficulties and troubles consequent on the use of fire-proof fluid, troubles which only appear when the canvas is completed and the effect of which it is impossible to foretell.

Hence it is advisable to use only those makes of canvas of proved efficiency and to avoid those heavily fire-proofed canvases which destroy the delicate priming and medium used in Continental scene painting. Misfortunes such as those described must be carefully avoided by the decorator or he may incur censure and experience unpleasant surprises.

L'Astuce Féminine

Our contract with Diaghileff expired in January, 1920, and from that time onwards we worked intermittently in Paris, Monte Carlo or London, at his request. Thus in February of that year we were summoned to Paris, to paint the scenery for the opera-ballet *L'Astuce Féminine*,[1] consisting of three acts, a drop-curtain and proscenium; the scene for the ballet *Pulcinella ;* and to repaint the scenes for *Schéhérazade*, *L'Oiseau de Feu* and other ballets.

For the purpose of this work Diaghileff took two large studios. In one I painted some of the scenes, while in the other my wife executed the remainder. Scene painting in Paris is a pleasant occupation, for there are plenty of huge studios specially fitted with every convenience. Each is provided with colours and brushes, and twice a week the studios are visited by the representatives of firms manufacturing colours, priming, medium, and so forth, while an unlimited number of assistants migrate from studio to studio according to the demand for their services. The climatic conditions, absence of fog and damp, contribute

---

[1] *Feminine Wiles.*

63

to quick drying, while the non-existence of a law requiring scenery to be fire-proofed relieves the decorator from the ever-present fear as to the success of his work. In short, one can concentrate on painting without having to solve abstruse technical questions.

French colours are very bright, very concentrated and available in many variations of tone, but are, unfortunately, less permanent than English makes, and fade quickly. The medium *colle de peau* is very convenient and retains a uniform strength though kept constantly heated, but it is thicker than so-called French glue, which cannot be obtained in Paris. Paris studios are usually so large that the half or quarter of one can be hired and will be found sufficient for the execution of a cloth measuring 60 × 40 feet, and it is not disturbing to work side by side with other artists. A studio always contains an upper gallery which allows one to judge the work in progress.

The scenery for *L'Astuce Féminine* was rather complicated in construction and contained a great number of tones with effects of light and shade. The designs for all three acts, painted in oils by Sert and suggesting the polished surface characteristic of ceramics, were impossible to reproduce in distemper, whatever the depth and strength of the colours. If it is important that the decorator should render the texture of a sketch, oil is one of the vehicles quite unsuitable for stage decoration, particularly where deep tones are concerned. All three acts underwent certain alterations and variations from the original sketches, through the intervention of Diaghileff, Sert and ourselves.

The most difficult part to paint proved to be the drapery of the drop-curtain and proscenium, which was very complicated in the drawing of the folds, the pattern and multifarious blending of tones. The scene for the second act, with its intricate perspective and many unrelated colours, required special attention for the production of a more or less concise impression. The scene for the third act, with its endless perspective of a town plunged in deep night, also needed much work on account of the intricacy of its drawing and bulkiness of construction. Later, the ballet which occurs in the third act was given separately under the title of *Cimarosiana*.

On account of this conception the scenes for *L'Astuce Féminine* must be classed with those of the pre-Bakst period, despite the attempt to afford them a modern spirit by brightening the colours. These scenes are among the least typical of the manner of stage decorations associated with the productions of the Diaghileff Company. From the technical point of view the execution proved to be quite satisfactory, despite the rather poor quality of the French canvas. At a later date the scenery was badly soaked by rain in Paris and had to be retouched in London and carefully restored in Monte Carlo, but I shall return to this later.

Pulcinella

The scenery for *Pulcinella*, painted from a sketch by Picasso, was executed (chiefly by my wife) at the same time as that for *L'Astuce Féminine*. Before deciding on one of his numerous designs, Picasso showed me the whole series and requested my opinion of them from the point of view of their theatrical effect. They were most interesting, but one seemed particularly suited for theatrical interpretation, and I told Picasso so. And, though Diaghileff preferred another sketch, Picasso told me that while working on his designs he involuntarily returned to the one that had attracted my attention. In the end this was decided on, and since the design, though no larger than a postcard, was clear and simple in all its details, the execution aroused no doubts, and was completed unusually quickly.

The design had been executed in *gouache*, and the coarse French canvas suited it admirably. Strong priming together with opaque and thick colours gave the desired effect. Picasso himself painted the central portion of the flat, but as usual did not depart from the details fixed by his sketch and checked all the stages of the painting from it. The scene succeeded very well from both technical and artistic viewpoints, and in its idea and execution must be regarded as one of the most interesting scenes of the Diaghileff Company. Although the tones were limited to white, grey, brown and blue, clearly outlined surfaces were used and the resulting impression was such that no other scene, whatever its degree of light and shade, pattern, contrast, and so forth, could be compared with it.

Continental Scene Painting

A few weeks later, a curious incident occurred during the dress rehearsal. The brown cut-cloth, to the astonishment of everyone, was found to be squared all over with grey lines similar to those of a Scotch plaid. On Diaghileff's enquiring as to where those American trousers came from, I could hardly believe the evidence of my eyes, nor give any immediate answer, knowing for certain that the cloth had been painted with a flat brown. An awkward pause ensued but, rushing on to the stage, I began dusting the grey lines while Picasso shouted joyously from the auditorium : " It is disappearing ! It is disappearing ! " to the accompaniment of unanimous laughter. The mystery was solved. It appeared that since the cloth had not been thoroughly dry when folded in the studio, mould had formed in the pattern of the folds. But after I had worked on the canvas with damp sawdust for some ten minutes, the " American trousers " were transformed into the plain brown cloth, to the relief of all present. This scene has never been repainted and, with the exception of an accident that occurred to the flats and a slight uniform fading, it keeps in splendid condition, having earned for Picasso a well-merited success.

At the same time, during our stay in Paris, the scene for *Schéhérazadé* was completely repainted and to it were added the long-lost wings for the columns, so necessary when setting the scene on a huge stage like that of the Grand Opera. The throne was again brought into the light of day and required much attention. The stage-cloth was renewed and, in general, everything carried out in accordance with Bakst's design.

The huge scene for *L'Oiseau de Feu*, with all its extra parts, which latter were rarely used, was again repainted, but with a slight heightening of tone as Diaghileff desired.

As there was a stock of fine vermilion in the studio, it was possible to repaint the sky of the back-cloth for the second act of *Contes Russes*, which it will be remembered could not be properly executed in London, owing to the difficulty of obtaining materials in wartime.

In general, the long days and dry climate of Paris, together with the comfortable conditions under which the work was carried out, permitted a considerable advance on the rate of production as compared with London.

PLATE 13

DESIGN BY VLADIMIR
POLUNIN FOR *POLKA*

The Sleeping Princess

This production, projected on so grandiose a scale and, on account of its complicated setting, entailing enormous expense, was short-lived and ended, as everyone knows, in a catastrophe.

The numerous acts of this ballet had been prepared in Paris ; some of the scenes were painted there and others in London. Bakst, like a field-marshal, sent out from his headquarters in Paris his instructions to the various studios. Those intended for us arrived by air mail, but his explanations were frequently contradictory. Three acts fell to our share but, as Bakst was not present, it was often difficult to fathom his meaning so that the work had to be held up pending explanations. To add to these difficulties it was found that the canvas, which had been purchased in great quantity, was worthless ; the priming fell off, while the colours peeled away and changed in tone before our eyes.

The fire-proofing with which the canvas had been treated was so strong that it destroyed or altered every tone, impaired the adhesiveness of the medium and absorbed even the slight moisture in the atmosphere due to a shower of rain. Although each piece was repainted five or six times, which improved the tone for a short while, it was impossible to obtain a satisfactory result. A change of medium, a strong solution of dextrin in place of French glue, did not improve the adhesiveness of the colours which daily precipitated a whitish deposit of unknown origin which covered the whole canvas like hoar frost. In spite of endless repainting there seemed to be no remedy, and this scene must be regarded as a complete failure from the technical standpoint.

But, compared with the sea of troubles which attended the production of this ballet, ours were a mere drop in the ocean. Nevertheless, the lesson learned was so instructive, that afterwards I was obliged to refuse commissions if the canvas supplied were of doubtful quality. But even when, after careful examination, the canvas proved satisfactory, a coarser and stronger medium—English size—was used and French glue never employed again on fire-proof canvases.

All this serves to show that not only are proper conditions from a technical point of view needed for the successsful execution of a scene, but a close collaboration between designer and decorator is imperative from the artistic standpoint. The executor in his work must, as it were, identify himself with the designer of the sketch so that he may produce not a mere copy but express the idea that inspired the artist.

La Tentation de la Bergère

The scene-painting studio at Monte Carlo, where my wife and I painted the scenery for *La Tentation de la Bergère*[1] and other ballets, is one of the best in Europe. The arrangements, staff, lighting, drying facilities and general accommodation are all that could be desired. The output of work in a studio where the climatic conditions are so favourable as to enable canvas to dry in winter quicker than in England in summer, can be brought to the highest pitch.

The setting for *La Tentation de la Bergère*, which consists of seven planes and numerous flats, can be classed with mixed types of scenery, that is one part is hung while the other consists of a complicated built construction. The difficulty of transporting bulky built parts, sometimes measuring 20 feet in length, the same trouble in erecting them on a stage in a short space of time, were not counterbalanced by the results obtained. It seemed to me that everything could have been simplified and reduced in size without detracting from the artistic effect of the whole.

The painting of the scene, executed from a coloured model prepared by Juan Gris, offered the same difficulties as in Matisse's model for *Le Chant du Rossignol*. But Gris's model was much more complicated on account of its general complexity, technique and combination of hanging with built scenery. The original *craché* technique of the walls, the seemingly endless number of scagiola surfaces led to minute work, while the intricacy of the drawing in general and of the built parts in particular required careful and precise execution.

Due praise must be accorded to the studio staff, who were most helpful in expediting and bringing the work to a successful issue. Economy of time in the studio was carried to such a degree that the preparatory work, which usually occupies a third of the time needed for the painting of a scene, was done so quickly that nothing was delayed.

The Faithful Shepherdess.

For example, the female staff, consisting of eight women, stretched a canvas on the floor in ten minutes, a proceeding which, performed under normal conditions by two workmen, would have required an hour or more. Again, the draughtsmen executed their work quickly and correctly, starting from both sides of the canvas at the same time, which considerably shortened the time taken for the all-important work of preparation.

The enormous area of the studio made it possible to work on several canvases simultaneously, while the model stage situated beneath it was most convenient, as the scenes could be hung there and the tones tested under actual lighting conditions, before being dispatched to the theatre proper. No incidents or unpleasant surprises occurred in connection with the painting of this scene, and when, the following year, it was given in London, no technical deficiencies whatever became evident.

Despite the coarseness of the canvas and the thick painting technique, the colours did not crack or peel away. The drapery, in order to add softness to the folds of a coarse canvas, was painted in aniline, so that this setting afforded not only a combination of hanging with built scenery, but a combination of painting vehicles—pigment and aniline.

La Colombe

Though the simple *maquette* constructed by Gris for *La Colombe* offered the usual difficulties of a model, these were counterbalanced by its interesting cubist construction, which reminded one, so far as the tones were concerned, of the scenery for *Pulcinella*. The painting technique was not so opaque as that employed for *La Tentation de la Bergère*, and the canvas did not appear to require a priming of unusual strength.

Gris personally did not make a single stroke of the brush on either scene, but for some reason decided to alter certain tones and the technique used in the process of painting *La Colombe*, although we advised him against doing so. Diaghileff seemed pleased with the progress of the work, and nothing foretold the complications to come.

Continental Scene Painting

The scene, despite the alterations, had an excellent appearance in the studio, but how different it appeared when set on the stage ! Instead of a delicate harmony of white, black, grey and blue, a dirty, brownish-grey tone pervaded the whole setting. Diaghileff was greatly displeased and desired it to be completely repainted. Nothing of the kind had ever happened before. Presently the origin of the transformation was explained. Owing to the peculiarities of construction of the scene and the strong lighting, the light penetrated the canvas from behind, completely changing the fundamental tones. For example, the walls, painted with practically pure white, appeared to be of a brownish-ochre colour, the black tones seemed reddish and so on, resulting in a vague cacophony.

When the scene was removed to the studio, the first thing done was to cover the back of the transparent canvases with thick neutral colours ; this arrested the penetration of light and consequent alteration in tone. But the French canvas was so coarse, dark in colour and thinly woven that it absorbed the usual priming and comparatively thin coat of colours, altering their relations and reducing their intensity. It was absurd to prime and repaint a scene just completed, and would have entailed much time and labour. Hence a method was devised which, though logical, had not been employed before.

We glazed the whole scene with a thin wash of aniline, which should neutralise the brownish tint without affecting the values. Blue aniline glazed over all the grey and black tones proved to be successful, although, as we have seen, distemper brushed over aniline undergoes unpleasant changes. Hence in a very short time, by a simple and complete retouching, all the tones were restored to their original delicate relation, and this somewhat unexpected solution of the difficulty must be regarded as a happy gift of fortune. Diaghileff was well pleased with the final result.

Since then, for safety, whenever we have used the coarse and thinly-woven French canvas it has, before painting, been primed twice, or washed over with neutral tones after the first priming. This method yielded good results. The scenery for *La Colombe* must be regarded as successful, both technically and artistically, although it has not been possible to test its durability, for the opera has not passed into the repertory of the company since its production at Monte Carlo.

Philémon et Baucis

Two scenes for *Philémon et Baucis* were painted from designs by Alexander Benois on canvas not only well primed, but also covered with a first coat of paint of a neutral colour. This manner of preparation proved to be not only very convenient and afforded a pleasing surface for painting on, but made it easier to obtain the impression of richness of material expressed in the design and, in general, to approach the technique of it. The unpleasant coarseness of French canvas, with its brownish tint, so difficult to overcome when the scene for *L'Astuce Féminine* was being executed, was by this means neutralised by the application of a primary coat of colour. The water-colour technique of Benois's designs, with its original treatment, was rendered on a coarse canvas as successfully as on a thin and expensive one.

The simplicity of his scenes, which were of the usual hanging type, their gay light and shade, produced the best results with the least complication. To know how to obtain a complete impression with a minimum number of planes is no small merit on the part of the designer.

It was very pleasant to work with Benois, a connoisseur of Russian theatrical art, an expert on old masters, and an eminent critic, owing to his charming personal qualities. Despite his great experience of the theatre he listened to our advice, and often acted upon it. Although he did not introduce anything new, he understood how to make use of stage possibilities, obtaining important results thereby. Both scenes were technically very well painted and met with Benois's high approval.

At this period many scenes were repainted simultaneously with the daily work on new productions. First, the scenes for Acts I. and III. of *L'Astuce Féminine* were overhauled. They were so much injured by rain that, not having been dried in time, the tones had disappeared at various places, while in the case of the back-cloth for Act I. the canvas had rotted in the most conspicuous parts. To sew in large pieces of new canvas and paint them so that the repairs are not noticeable is one of the most difficult operations in scene painting. It was

71

not that the whole cloth needed repainting, but, to blend faded tones with those on new patches, using the same technique, is by no means so easy as it may seem.

Again, to remove the huge stains on the other cloths offered no little difficulty. But this time the result was so successful that when the scenes were hung in the theatre I asked Diaghileff to try and discover the new patches ; after a long examination he relinquished the task, but when I showed him the back of a cloth he was astonished to see the numerous large square patches of new canvas ; so the importance of the tailor's and restorer's tasks was justified.

The scenery for *Cléopâtre* which, it will be recalled, was injured by water vapour during the first season of the Diaghileff Company at the Coliseum, and afterwards by rain, needed thorough attention. The particular difficulty in this case arose from the scene's having been painted in aniline, the retouching of which is very difficult ; the process required may be compared to the treatment for water stains. Not only had the damaged parts to be renewed, but the whole scene, which had faded considerably in the space of six years, required to be refreshed.

If all the peculiarities of aniline colours, the bad results obtained from their admixture, and the limited number of standard shades are taken into consideration, it must be admitted that the task is a thankless one, where the slightest mistake or blot at the wrong place may damage the whole cloth. However, the scenery for *Cléopâtre* was successfully restored, and remained in good condition until the ballet was taken from the repertory.

The scenery for *Daphnis et Chloé*, a ballet which had not been given for a considerable period, was also partly repainted on the stage at Monte Carlo. This scene, like other early works of Bakst, had suffered mainly in the ultramarine and other deep tones ; the renovation of these, however, occasioned no difficulties and was effected in a few hours before the raising of the curtain

Le Lac des Cygnes,[1] a delicate and beautiful scene designed by C. Korovin, had to be reduced in size ; and to cut a medium-sized scene out of huge cut-cloths and network necessitates considerable

[1] *The Swan Lake.*

PLATE 14

MODEL OF SETTING DESIGNED
BY VLADIMIR POLUNIN FOR USE
WITH BLACK VELVET SURROUND

calculation, and is by no means easy, particularly when it is remembered that each new seam requires to be painted in skilful imitation of the faded tones of a work twenty years old. The scene had remained folded up for many years and was almost an antique. It was impossible not to admire its technical completeness and withhold tribute to the knowledge and understanding possessed by the masters of the end of the last century. The delicate combination of tones, good taste and voluntary complexity of drawing afforded the impression of something as fragile as Venetian lace and harmonised exactly with the spirit of the ballet. And though its conception did not accord with present-day standards, it had many praiseworthy qualities.

This quaint painting, executed on a splendid Russian canvas, despite the lapse of twenty years—which is nearly double the normal life of a scene—was in such excellent condition [1] that it could have been used on the stage at any time without need for repainting or repairs.

To convey some idea of the diversity of the work carried on daily in the scenic studios of the Diaghileff Company, it may be of interest to reproduce a portion of my diary when working at Monte Carlo.

Friday.	Began two pieces of *Cléopâtre*.
Saturday.	Finished two pieces of *Cléopâtre*.
	Primed two canvases for a new ballet.
Monday.	Began two pieces of *Les Femmes de Bonne Humeur*.
Tuesday.	Finished the two pieces of *Les Femmes de Bonne Humeur*.
	Began carpet and canopy of *Cléopâtre*.
	Revised *Les Sylphides*.
	Began cut-cloth for *Les Sylphides*.
Wednesday.	Finished carpet and canopy of *Cléopâtre*.
	Began cut-cloth of *Cléopâtre*.
Thursday.	Finished cut-cloth of *Cléopâtre*.
	Began back-cloth of *Cléopâtre*.

[1] This statement is of great importance in view of what I have been informed regarding the scenery stores at the Royal Opera House, Covent Garden, where a scene, after being carefully rolled up for some ten years, is frequently found to be unfit for use.

Friday.   Finished back-cloth of *Cléopâtre*.

Began and finished two tents for *Prince Igor*.

Bridge for *Le Tricorne*.

Repaired back-cloth for Act I. of *L'Astuce Féminine*.

Saturday.   Began and finished two tents for *Prince Igor*.

Began bull and veil for *Cléopâtre*.

Began drop-curtain for *La Tentation de la Bergère*.

Monday.   Finished bull for *Cléopâtre*.

Summoned to Diaghileff.

Began back-cloth for Act I. of *L'Astuce Féminine*.

Began and finished stage-cloth for *Petrouchka*.

Began and finished cutting of canvas for Acts I. and II. of *Le Lac des Cygnes*.

The above shows clearly how, according to the demands of the performances to be given, the work of keeping the existing scenery in order is carried on simultaneously with the preparation and painting of scenes for new ballets, so that the number of finished scenes depends partly on the space available on the studio floor.

A working day of eight hours in a studio must be carefully planned out in order to be productive. This responsibility rests on the organising powers of the decorator, who must contrive that the mental strain of painting is carefully alternated with such purely physical hard work as the stretching and priming of canvas, wielding of huge brushes, and continual walking to and fro. A faulty manner of holding the brush, a wrong position of the body, a constant unnecessary returning to the same place while working, all lead to bodily fatigue, which adversely affects the progress of the work.

The value of organisation and distribution of work cannot be over-emphasised, for without this care work which, properly carried out, should not take more than one day may be continued far into the night ; while, on the other hand, it may be impossible to work at all another day, not because there is no work to do, but simply because nothing has been planned out in advance.

A well-trained staff of assistants and workmen greatly aids in the simplification of the work, and affords good results. A clever assistant working side by side with the master does not affect the general style of his painting, while a trained workman can carry out independently such preparatory work as stretching, priming, folding of the canvas, and so on, without the constant supervision of the master, who is thus free to devote himself uninterruptedly to his principal work of painting the scene.

The Drop Curtain for the Russian Ballet Season at the Coliseum, 1925

In order to separate the performance of the Diaghileff Company from the varied programme of a music-hall, I was commissioned to design a drop-curtain which should at once effect this purpose and be symbolical of the spirit of the Russian Ballet. Now the designing of a drop-curtain is one of the most difficult problems, and was further complicated in the present instance owing to its having to fulfil a dual purpose.

Having decided on a purely Russian conception with balanced masses and tones which should produce the effect of a decorative flat surface, I began to prepare the cloth, a huge canvas measuring 60 × 33 feet. This had to be softly primed so that the grain, which contributed to the silkiness of the painting, should not be obscured. Despite the apparent intricacy of the composition, which consisted of a horseman, mountains, trees and so forth, the drawing was quickly transferred to the canvas, since the outlines had been simplified to the maximum degree.

The fundamental tones—red, white, light greyish-blue and green— were carefully chosen in accordance with the sketch and painted in flat masses with fairly thin colours. Afterwards a slight shading was introduced, being laid on again with thin colours, the tones corresponding to those of the different masses. This at once removed any suggestion of a poster and afforded a certain softness and slightly perceptible relief. On the other hand, the application of a damp sponge to the waves, clouds and hills gave the delicate gradation of a painting on silk. The minute details, such as those on the horseman, bushes and so forth, and the more important shadows were painted with practically dry tempera colours, for this rubbing in leads to that precision and softness necessary for the transition from light to shade.

The only difficulty was the execution of the sky, which had to be painted in gold, for all attempts at mixing bronze powder with different mediums led to such poor results as to promise failure, the reason being that the fire-proof fluid blackened the gold and destroyed the adhesiveness of the medium. Gold, so beautiful with distemper, when thinly applied with gelatine again instantly darkened and acquired a bluish-green tint, which marred the whole effect of the curtain. Other mediums, satisfactory in that they more or less kept the tone, had to be discarded because they gave an oily shade of faded gold quite opposed to the impression I desired. Unable to counteract the corrosive action of the fire-proof fluid on the gold, I was forced to use gold size, which did not blacken, adhered well and was sufficiently light in colour. Its strength and brilliance reminded one of the gold used in the illumination of missals and harmonised perfectly with the general style of the design.

Regarded as a whole, the dimensions of the composition and manner of execution, devoid of all unnecessary detail, produced a complete impression. And at the lighting rehearsal both Diaghileff and the direction of the Coliseum expressed their approval of the drop-curtain, which was received with enthusiasm by the audience.

Soirées de Paris

A new theatrical enterprise, inaugurated at Paris, in 1924, by the Comte E. de Beaumont, promised to be interesting both from the point of view of the productions planned and the choice of the dancers and painters to be associated with them. A. Derain, G. Braque, Picasso, Marie Laurencin and myself were commissioned to design the various scenes. The direction put two studios at our disposal so that work could be begun simultaneously on three canvases, the preparatory work being carried out in one studio, the painting in the other.

Salade

Salade, designed by Georges Braque in the form of a *maquette* and consisting of three parallel planes only, offered no technical difficulties in its execution, but the subtle scale of tones and a certain vagueness of outline required to be handled with delicacy and attention. In this scene the *matière* of the painting and the quality of the surface played an important part. For the first time, two kinds of canvases were purposely used in the same scene, because the cut-cloth in the *maquette* had a rougher surface than the other planes ; this combination produced a certain charm.

For the cut-cloth a coarse canvas was selected, strong priming used, and the painting executed with thick colours. The rest of the scene was painted on thin white canvas with almost a water-colour technique in accordance with the *maquette*. Each outline of the *maquette* consisted of numerous broken lines apparently correcting one another, and this effect, at Braque's request, was reproduced exactly. The delicate colouring of the landscape and of the walls, with their light greyish-white, bluish and brownish gradations of tone, was so successful as to render completely the delicate charm of the designer's colouring. The rough *matière* of the bright pink cut-cloth in the foreground afforded the necessary accent and placed, as it were, the chromatic scale of the whole scene on a firm basis.

Although this scene, relatively speaking, was not of large dimensions, the planes being few in number, its execution required much time and work ; nevertheless, the result was most successful in every way.

Le Beau Danube

The second scene carried out was that for *Le Beau Danube*, designed by me, which, intended for a large number of dancers, required a greater depth of stage. The theme of the ballet necessitated the evocation of a particular period—the Second Empire—as recorded in the drawings of Constantin Guys. This scene was painted in a purely water-colour technique in accordance with the design, the general chromatic scale of delicate values producing the effect of a slightly tinted engraving set in a pale pink mount and framed in gold. The method of using the sponge was applied in every part of this scene in order to give the softness and airiness characteristic of the sketch.

Les Roses

This scene, planned from a small water-colour by Marie Laurencin, which represented a fragile lady on horseback and some scarlet drapery, produced the effect of a piquant circus. The wide wings representing drapery made the stage smaller in accordance with the choreographic requirements. A water-colour technique was used as being the only one capable of rendering the feminine charm of Laurencin's work. The difficult combination of pink, scarlet, blue and black tones proved very effective on the canvas, yet this scene, despite its small dimensions and apparent simplicity, took much longer to execute than at first imagined.

Gigue

Derain's sketch for *Gigue* was simple and clear, but required different techniques in the execution of the several planes. The back-cloth, a sky with a gradation of bluish tones, was painted in water-colour technique ; the other portion was executed with thick paint on a rougher canvas. This time Derain, although present during the painting of the scene, did not attempt a single stroke of the brush. Everything had been settled by him in his sketch and nothing was altered during the painting of the scene. Bluish-black and white tones, at once intense and exceedingly soft, afforded a clearly expressed harmony and provided an excellent background for the brightly-coloured costumes of the dancers.

A real statue, painted black, introduced by Derain, though a somewhat risky innovation for the stage, did not spoil the impression, but accorded an unexpected, austere aspect to the whole.

In March, 1926, I received a telephone message from Charles B. Cochran, who had purchased the scenery for *Gigue*, requesting me to enlarge and repaint some of the canvases which had become damaged in storage. It was difficult to repaint the cobalt of the sky with the

PLATE 15

DESIGN BY VLADIMIR POLUNIN
FOR *LE BEAU DANUBE*

English colours available. In fact, there is no cobalt on the market, so that a combination of azure blue, white, and so on was used in its place. All the flats, despite transport and reframing, were in good condition.

Mercure

The scenery designed by Picasso for *Mercure*, a ballet in three acts, consisted of a series of screens of intense and definite colour bound together in a masterly manner. The designs, done in pastel, were no larger than a match-box. The screens served as a background for wire structures, introduced for the first time on the stage. Picasso took, as usual, an active part in the execution of the work, examining the composition of the tones and the process of the painting.

The greyish-black colours, with their central portion of the bright tones of water-plants, of the first act, the beautiful brick-red colour of the second act, and the creamy, ostrich-egg-like tone of the last act required opaque painting in order to reproduce the effect of pastel. A rough canvas was selected and strongly primed, and the colours, being applied thickly, gave the mat appearance of the medium of the sketch. The use of two studios enabled the three scenes to be completed in a comparatively short space of time, although due time and attention were given to each canvas.

Working in collaboration with Picasso was very pleasant, as on former occasions, thanks to his interesting innovations and unchangeable decisions. Doubts and variations from the original design are always detrimental to the work of the executor, since they impair the freshness of the painting and lead to all manner of disquieting surprises.

The drop-curtain and proscenium for *Soirées de Paris* were also painted from sketches by Picasso. The unusual pastel technique of the design, the softness of the outline and mat quality of the surface were most difficult to reproduce in distemper. A dry glazing of the painting, akin to pastel technique, and rubbing were used in those parts of the design which required it. The wide range of shades possessed by pastel, the peculiarity of its technique, the difference between a rubbed pastel and one directly drawn, were extremely difficult to interpret in distemper. It was no easy task to render the bluish-green and creamy-red tones of the design, quite apart from its technique, and effect their cohesion. The wire-like outlines of figures were traced over the paintings by Picasso himself and, at his request, softened by rubbing, as he found them slightly crude. At last, after assiduous efforts, the work was brought to a successful conclusion, and this curtain was acclaimed one of the most interesting attractions of the *Soirées de Paris*.

All the above-mentioned scenes proved to be painted satisfactorily from both artistic and technical viewpoints, and free from the accidents and defects that so often attend on the work of scene painting.

Scenery for Russian Cabaret

In the intervals of work for the Diaghileff Company, I was commissioned to design and execute various scenes of small dimensions for the Russian Cabaret *The Eager Centipede*, produced by T. Komisarjevsky at the Prince's Gallery ; for the Cabaret of B. Evelinoff and V. Rosing at the Prince's Restaurant in 1921 ; and for Balieff's *Chauve Souris* in 1925.

For Komisarjevsky, I designed and painted *Spanish Serenade*, *The Drum Major* and *Wooden Toys* (*Troika*), which for the most part consisted of a backcloth with side-pieces.

For Rosing, I designed and carried out *Vanka Tanka*, *English Porcelain*, *The Volga Boatmen*, *The Drum Major* and others.

For Balieff, I undertook the scene for *The Two Huntsmen* and the Chamber set for *Gypsy Party*.

All these settings were achieved without technical errors, despite the enforced rapidity of their execution. The planning of scenes for use in Cabaret is most interesting, but demands considerable imagination and the most assiduous application, for this type of entertainment requires a constant stream of ideas. Frequently, a complete programme number is evolved from the artist's design.

Nothing could afford greater contrast than the variety of the scenes which make up such an entertainment. Scenes based on humour, others conceived in a naïve, almost childlike simplicity, alternate with numbers

MODEL OF SETTING DESIGNED
BY VLADIMIR POLUNIN FOR USE
WITH BLACK VELVET SURROUND

PLATE 16

in the most serious vein. In general, work for Cabaret, despite its inherent difficulties, such as the miniature size of the cloths, proximity of the scene to the spectator, and kinematographic rapidity of presentation, is the most pleasant of tasks.

To the same category of scenes belong *The Cockatoo's Holiday* (1922), which I painted for Leonid Massine ; the settings for *Prince Igor*, *Le Spectre de la Rose*, *Dutch Ballet* and so on, designed and executed by me for A. Gavriloff's foreign tour, also the design for a Negro Ballet which he gave in America ; and the scene for ballet, *The Postman*, which I executed for Lydia Lopokova at the Coliseum in 1925.

Surroundings

At the end of 1925, Henry Crocker, the stage manager of the London Coliseum, asked me to solve a rather difficult technical problem. The constant use of black or grey curtains during the performances had become so monotonous that it was necessary to break up the dark area by the addition of coloured masses. A series of models was prepared for this purpose, and two of them (one designed by my wife), executed in 1926, succeeded very well. The remainder were held over for subsequent execution.

Since I mention coloured models and not sketches, it may seem that I acted contrary to the instructions I have laid down regarding the use of the former. This is the explanation : A sketch by itself was found to be insufficient in this case, on account of the important part to be played by velvet, with its peculiar surface. I therefore found it advisable to manipulate the coloured masses on actual pieces of this material. Again, from the employer's point of view, a coloured model on velvet gave him a complete idea of the effect intended.

Stage sets of velvet generally mask in perfectly, allowing the designer complete freedom to proceed with the coloured masses regardless of dimensions. At the same time the cost of such surroundings is considerably less than that of a full scene, since the same velvet surroundings can serve for innumerable settings. The question of economy effected a demand for such sets, and this method was much in use by the *Chauve Souris* and other cabarets, but only in the form of flats ; whereas it can be employed in a much broader sense by applying all the elements of hanging and built scenery to the velvet background. Thus one may often obtain interesting and unexpected results impossible in an ordinary fully-developed scene.

This style of simplified scenery will, I believe, largely supplant the complicated settings of the past.

General Index

General Index

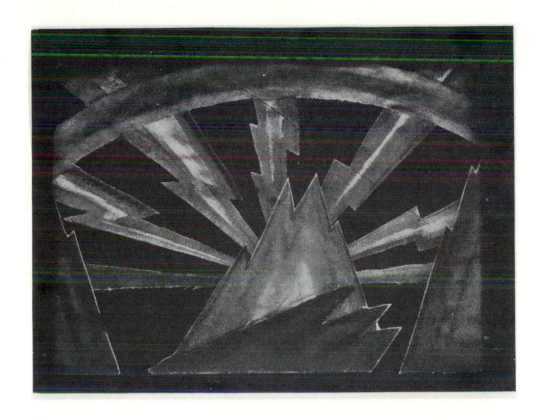

PLATE 16

MODEL OF SETTING DESIGNED
BY VLADIMIR POLUNIN FOR USE
WITH BLACK VELVET SURROUND

interpret in distemper. It was no easy task to render the bluish-green and creamy-red tones of the design, quite apart from its technique, and effect their cohesion. The wire-like outlines of figures were traced over the paintings by Picasso himself and, at his request, softened by rubbing, as he found them slightly crude. At last, after assiduous efforts, the work was brought to a successful conclusion, and this curtain was acclaimed one of the most interesting attractions of the *Soirées de Paris*.

All the above-mentioned scenes proved to be painted satisfactorily from both artistic and technical viewpoints, and free from the accidents and defects that so often attend on the work of scene painting.

Scenery for Russian Cabaret

In the intervals of work for the Diaghileff Company, I was commissioned to design and execute various scenes of small dimensions for the Russian Cabaret *The Eager Centipede*, produced by T. Komisarjevsky at the Prince's Gallery ; for the Cabaret of B. Evelinoff and V. Rosing at the Prince's Restaurant in 1921 ; and for Balieff's *Chauve Souris* in 1925.

For Komisarjevsky, I designed and painted *Spanish Serenade*, *The Drum Major* and *Wooden Toys* (*Troika*), which for the most part consisted of a backcloth with side-pieces.

For Rosing, I designed and carried out *Vanka Tanka*, *English Porcelain*, *The Volga Boatmen*, *The Drum Major* and others.

For Balieff, I undertook the scene for *The Two Huntsmen* and the Chamber set for *Gypsy Party*.

All these settings were achieved without technical errors, despite the enforced rapidity of their execution. The planning of scenes for use in Cabaret is most interesting, but demands considerable imagination and the most assiduous application, for this type of entertainment requires a constant stream of ideas. Frequently, a complete programme number is evolved from the artist's design.

Nothing could afford greater contrast than the variety of the scenes which make up such an entertainment. Scenes based on humour, others conceived in a naïve, almost childlike simplicity, alternate with numbers

English colours available. In fact, there is no cobalt on the market, so that a combination of azure blue, white, and so on was used in its place. All the flats, despite transport and reframing, were in good condition.

Mercure

The scenery designed by Picasso for *Mercure*, a ballet in three acts, consisted of a series of screens of intense and definite colour bound together in a masterly manner. The designs, done in pastel, were no larger than a match-box. The screens served as a background for wire structures, introduced for the first time on the stage. Picasso took, as usual, an active part in the execution of the work, examining the composition of the tones and the process of the painting.

The greyish-black colours, with their central portion of the bright tones of water-plants, of the first act, the beautiful brick-red colour of the second act, and the creamy, ostrich-egg-like tone of the last act required opaque painting in order to reproduce the effect of pastel. A rough canvas was selected and strongly primed, and the colours, being applied thickly, gave the mat appearance of the medium of the sketch. The use of two studios enabled the three scenes to be completed in a comparatively short space of time, although due time and attention were given to each canvas.

Working in collaboration with Picasso was very pleasant, as on former occasions, thanks to his interesting innovations and unchangeable decisions. Doubts and variations from the original design are always detrimental to the work of the executor, since they impair the freshness of the painting and lead to all manner of disquieting surprises.

The drop-curtain and proscenium for *Soirées de Paris* were also painted from sketches by Picasso. The unusual pastel technique of the design, the softness of the outline and mat quality of the surface were most difficult to reproduce in distemper. A dry glazing of the painting, akin to pastel technique, and rubbing were used in those parts of the design which required it. The wide range of shades possessed by pastel, the peculiarity of its technique, the difference between a rubbed pastel and one directly drawn, were extremely difficult to